Destin. Unknown

What Happens to Us When We Die? People from Around the World Weigh in On Humanity's Greatest Unsolved Mystery

By: John H. Clark III

www.JohnClarkBooks.com

Copyright © 2015 John H. Clark III

Publishing services provided by **Archangel Ink**

ISBN: 1942761198
ISBN-13: 978-1-942761-19-8

Foreword

The question of life—its meaning, significance, and purpose—is a question that all people, cultures, and individuals face at some point in time. The power of this very act contains within it the ability to transform us all, to change our emotions and the course of our lives. It is a seed that is born inside us, growing as we grow, waiting to blossom, and its blooms are the actions, expressions, and creations of our lives.

Contemplating our existence, life, and death, both personally and as a whole, can have a profound impact on how we live our lives. It is one of the most difficult and challenging concepts that everyone faces at some point, or many points, in one's lifetime. I have reflected many times on this concept, and it has been an ever-evolving understanding of my spirit's journey—a journey that will be an eternity of continual growth and expansion. A constant state of discovery, learning, and evolving as our consciousness opens to more love and peace that flows harmoniously with all in this universe and beyond.

My own understanding and exploration of these important questions and the topics of life, death, life after death, God, heaven, and hell has been in a constant state of evolution. It's been an evolution of the spirit as my personal search and journey has brought many new, unique, and special experiences that have helped to expand my understanding and acceptance of what could arguably be some of the most sensitive questions or topics that man is faced with.

I have always felt, from a very early age, more spiritual than religious. I can always remember a feeling from my childhood that something just wasn't quite right with a lot of the information, beliefs, and ways of the world I was exposed to. I felt deep pain, sadness, and frustration that much of what I witnessed or experienced didn't always flow with a deep sense of love, peace, respect, and honor of our true oneness of mankind and our relationship with the Divine. I can remember questioning, heart aching, and crying for people who were not treated with equal love and respect. Feelings that I think we all feel to some degree at our core, and, depending on our life experiences, are felt profoundly at different times and lead us to reflecting, questioning, and striving to find our own personal truth.

Having been raised in a loving Catholic household, I was part of a routine that I can now see in many ways had many positive effects, as any routine provides. There is a closeness and a consistency to our actions and lives that can bring comfort on many levels. It provides the opportunity to share in a group or collective experience. With consistency, a routine, in a way, saves us from the fears of change and a real exploration of outside belief systems and structures that we build our lives around. We listen, learn, and take action on what others have decided to be "true," or state as the real "truth," instead of letting our spirits be the explorers they were meant to be–on a journey to discover, engage, learn, and grow in a truly incredible universe that "True Source" or God created for us to explore as the unique creations we are.

For most of man's existence, awakening or advancements in consciousness seems to come through pain or difficult life lessons. It is these very serious–and in many cases, tragic–exchanges of people and cultures that have been the doorway to a deeper understanding, caring, and willingness to change.

I have often reflected on the idea: "What if the Ten Commandments had been written in the affirmative or positive?" Just think if man acted the majority of the time from a place of love and peace, instead of fear. Instead of a list of "Thou Shall Not," what if we had all been raised with an understanding and guidance that True Source or God created us to be totally loving, accepting, and unlimited in positive creation? What if we had been taught that a united relationship with God in co-creation of our spirit's desire would express itself in loving, peaceful, caring, and collaborative ways with others that make a difference in the world?

Throughout my life, I, too, experienced a series of personal challenges, which cracked open the door to my consciousness and its desire to expand, develop, and grow to new heights. Of course, at the time, I had to deal with the fear and difficult feelings that were a part of many of those experiences. Opening my feelings and doing what I could to work through those challenges was a part of my consciousness learning and expanding. As Einstein said, "No problem can be solved from the level of consciousness that created it." It is only through higher realizations and deeper insights to our experiences that we have the potential for growth, and ultimately for making different choices and decisions, having integrated new learning and knowledge.

Some of those events led me to discover what at the time was a concept called New Age. We now take this as more mainstream, because of many people's interest in quantum physics, science, psychology, and the craze of self-help, as well as an interest and desire to better understand ourselves and the world we live in. I was fascinated by what I read, and having studied in college and received a second degree in psychology, the area of the mind has always fascinated me. It was an interesting complement to my first degree, where I was a business major with an emphasis in marketing, sales, and advertising.

Over the years, a thirst for learning and discovery, along with these experiences that at the time felt unique and out of the norm, expanded into a deeper understanding of the immensity of the universe and the world we live in. Little by little, my spirit and consciousness was growing—a concept and idea that I know will continue and exist forever, as we truly are eternal immortal spirits.

This connection of the spirit, mind, and body—a trilogy working in unison to help us maneuver in and through the world to experience and gain a better understanding of a variety of perspectives—led me on a journey of learning and discovering information that helped in expanding my consciousness, and also deepened my appreciation of life and the world we live in.

This journey led me to discover information and gain an understanding of past lives and reincarnation; the immensity of the universe and the spirit's journey as now expressed in quantum physics, which includes concepts of parallel universes and different dimensions that our spirit or soul makes in its learning adventure; and the importance of synchronicity as our natural internal guidance system of intuition, our own GPS that helps us to connect and interact with those that we are meant to as part of our life's path, purpose, and destiny.

For me, earth is a life school–an opportunity for our spirit to experience and learn. A place where on this journey we have the chance to become aware of our life purpose, which for me is using our True Source- or God-given gifts and talents working collaboratively with others to make a difference in the world.

I have always been one to believe that whatever I know today is only the consciousness and awareness that I have at this moment, and I hope in each moment to come that my consciousness continues to expand, bringing me to higher levels of understanding. Maybe it is this basis that has allowed me to be open to many different concepts and philosophies, many of which at the time were, and even today are, difficult for the "masses" to understand and accept. I, too, have held on to many beliefs, even when they no longer served me and could have been discarded in exchange for new beliefs that would have served me better, but this is a part of all of our journeys as we continue to experience, learn, and grow. It has been a process—a process that I hope will continue to evolve in a smooth flow that allows and supports more peace, love, gratitude, and compassion in each moment.

How can a finite mind understand the infinite True Source or God that is all knowing, all loving, and complete in its acceptance and understanding, with its immeasurable desire for us to truly live as the eternal spirits we were created to be? This loving True Source or God is ever present and always available to listen, acknowledge, and interact with us twenty-four hours a day, seven days a week, for every thought is a prayer that is listened to. The spirit never rests or ceases, but is in constant communication with the Divine.

As my consciousness continues to learn, expand, and grow, I have moved from different points of view of many of these concepts of life and death, what happens to us after we die, and heaven and hell. Though I believe and know that our souls or spirits are immortal and continue into other realms of existence that contain more peace, love, and incredible beauty, that same knowledge does not always take away the fear about the way in which one will make the transition—death—or the sadness, hurt, or fear of losing loved ones, both family and friends.

These are human emotions and part of the human experience to feel, deal with, and integrate as part of our soul's journey. We are forever together, even though the "form" of the energy has changed, and in time I believe our souls will remember how to connect and share with our loved ones both here and beyond in new ways.

Just like cell phones that send text messages, our capabilities will expand and we will have gained more access to what has always been available, but not accessible, within our current understanding. Just as fire was a phenomenon that existed for millions of years, it took man's consciousness opening up to this concept to allow him to access it.

It was an honor and very special pleasure when John Clark asked me to share my thoughts on this subject. It provided a special opportunity for me to reflect on my spirit's journey and remember many significant times and points in my life. I can see that from childhood until this very moment, my spirit has been seeking to better understand, grow, and learn the importance of spending time reflecting or meditating on such important ideas.

As we move away from fear and denial, we can break through our own barriers, belief systems, and those that the world holds as true at certain points in time. As with all things, man's coming to his own consciousness will continue, and we can only hope that it can more readily come from a place of personal choice, love, caring, and compassion.

Releasing fear and judgment, which is a gift in and of itself and is the transformer of worlds as we know them, provides the opportunity for rebirth—a rebirth of ideas and a true renaissance in our time that is being experienced around the world at this very moment while we all learn to love and live in gratitude and harmony with one another.

Susan R. Mann
La Jolla, California

Susan is a graduate of Cal-State University, Fullerton, a spiritual seeker and contributor to the books, *Your Soaring Phoenix*, *Evolving Women's Consciousness: Dialogues with 21st Century Women*, and *Spiritual Gurus, Spiritual Paths: Your Choice*. Susan is uniting Camino authors globally in a new book with the working title, *Our Collective Camino*, a project designed to share the power of pilgrimage and the spirit of the Camino, as well as writing her own personal synchronistic story in *Bo Camiño—Beyond Coincidence: My Spanish Trails Of Synchronicity*.

Table of Contents

Introduction 1

Chapter 1: Missy Walters 4

Chapter 2: Jean Francois Fejoz 8

Chapter 3: Laurie Bryan Larson 13

Chapter 4: Andres Harnisch 16

Chapter 5: Jennifer Fitzgerald 23

Chapter 6: Alf B. Dahl 27

Chapter 7: Luanne Edwards Gordon 31

Chapter 8: Koi Hatchootucknee 35

Chapter 9: Suzy Ortiz 42

Chapter 10: Ellory Bockting 48

Chapter 11: Sara Zanini 54

Chapter 12: Brett Sailors 57

Chapter 13: Paula J. 61

Chapter 14: Robert Forrester 66

Chapter 15: Amber Iversen 71

Chapter 16: Swami Yogeshwaranand Bharti 75

Chapter 17: Brooke Lewis 78

Chapter 18: Linda Meadors 85

Chapter 19: Andy Hermosillo 90

Chapter 20: Stacey Kelsey 95

Chapter 21: Ingeborg Baltussen 97

Chapter 22: Jim M. 102

Chapter 23: Vanessa Rivera 108

Chapter 24: Salma Falah 114

Chapter 25: Claude Tranchant 117

Chapter 26: Randy Dyer 120

Chapter 27: Michele Watson 126

Chapter 28: Janet Schwind 130

Chapter 29: Amanda Sanchez 135

Chapter 30: Nabeel Sakhnini 138

Chapter 31: Barbara S. 144

Chapter 32: Whit Crandall 148

Chapter 33: Nancy Harvey 150

Chapter 34: Tony Barrio 155

Chapter 35: Susanne Sims 160

Chapter 36: Bruce Welch 167

Chapter 37: Lucía Miguel Bores 171

Chapter 38: Linda Altum 176

Chapter 39: Stefan Emunds 179

Chapter 40: Dr. Heather Rivera 182

Chapter 41: Kenya Cluff 186

Conclusion 190

Get My Books FREE 195

A Small Favor to Ask 196

About the Author 197

Introduction

Dying is a part of life.

If one is to live, one must also someday die. No question about it. It's one of nature's laws—a law of the universe, God's plan, the cycle of all living things.

Like the famous verse in the Bible book of Ecclesiastes: "There is a time for everything…a time to be born and a time to die…" (New International Version, Eccl. 3)

We are born. We live. We die. Of this, there can be no doubt. But what happens after we leave this life? This is perhaps the biggest and most controversial question of all time.

Why are we here? What is our purpose? What is the meaning of our existence? These are all good questions having to do with living. Finding a satisfactory answer to those types of questions can make the sometimes bumpy road between birth and death ride a little smoother for some people. We humans like things to make sense—everything neat and tidy, fitting into a nice little box in a way we can understand. And there certainly are lots of different answers and opinions to be found about the meaning and purpose of life.

This book, however, seeks to find answers to the question of what happens when we reach the end of the road.

Is this the only life we get? Or is there such a thing as second chances when it comes to life? None of the people I know who have died have ever come back to clue me in. At least, I haven't seen or talked to any of them. Are they swirling around somewhere in some other dimension, watching over me or some other loved one? You know, like guardian angels.

Are they up in heaven with God and Jesus and their angels, basking in some kind of eternal glory? Or maybe—especially when it comes to a lot of the people I've known and hung out with—sweating it out somewhere else, in a less pleasant, more uncomfortable location?

That complete stranger who crosses your path, wrapping you in a sense of déjà vu like you've seen them somewhere else before, known them somewhere else before, or been with them someplace else before. Have you? Did you?

Is death, as one person I talked to describes it, simply lights out? That's it. No more. Nowhere else to go. Nothing else to see. Just the long sleep.

Or is there something beyond our experience of death?

One thing I've learned over the years is that if I have a question about something, somebody else probably has the same question. So, to try to get a sense of what others think about life after death, and also to maybe find some answers that would make sense to me, I interviewed as wide a variety of people as I could find, from as wide a variety of places as I could manage. People from all across the United States and beyond. Some were in-person interviews, some were phone-call interviews, some were interviews conducted by e-mail, and some were Skype interviews.

And the results were fascinating. When I interviewed people for my very first book, *Finding God: An Exploration of Spiritual Diversity in America's Heartland*, it was amazing how willing people were to open their hearts and bare their souls, to let me into their lives for a while and let me have a look around at some highly personal stuff. When I started that project with the interview of a produce grower and seller outside the downtown courthouse in tiny San Saba, Texas, it quickly became apparent that the stories I was going to get would be much more than simply what people thought about the existence of God. They started telling me about incredible, life-changing events, both tragic and triumphant, that helped shape, change, or reinforce their beliefs.

And the same thing happened again this time. I spoke with dozens of believers and nonbelievers: men, women, old, young, atheist, agnostic, Christian, Buddhist, Hindu, and Muslim. People from all over the United States—East Coast, West Coast, Deep South, Southwest, Midwest, Northeast—and from across the world: Australia, Cuba, El Salvador, England, France, Germany, Holland, India, Israel, Italy, Morocco, Norway, Spain, Thailand.

An amazing experience.

It's remarkable and humbling when people open up to you so candidly. It is extremely moving to ask someone highly personal questions and have them look you in the eye and pour out their heart about a subject like their own death. Just amazing.

I think you will find these stories as fascinating as I do, and hopefully, you will see something of yourself somewhere in these words and maybe find an answer to a question you have about death, dying, and what comes next.

Chapter 1:

Missy Walters

> *"I just believe that people should try to live with no regrets, so that dying isn't an awful thing."*

Life after death is not something that Alaska kindergarten teacher Missy Walters particularly believes in. No heaven or hell. No reward for good behavior, nor eternal damnation for bad.

But she does believe that the human spirit survives death somehow, either here on Earth or elsewhere.

"I hope that there's life after death—I think it's a good idea—but I don't 100 percent believe in it," Ms. Walters, thirty-four, says.

"I hope that there's some kind of peaceful afterlife for people to live in, but what I don't think there is, is some kind of eternal purgatory. If there is a God that is all loving and all understanding, I don't think that people go to hell.

"I don't exactly believe in God, in the traditional sense, and that's a hard thing to say. I'm not saying I don't believe in God, but definitely not in the traditional sense.

"I always describe myself not as religious, but as a little bit spiritual, and I guess what I hope is that in some capacity, your spirit lives on…whether that be in people that you care about or places that you care about.

"Nature is a big part of my life, and a big part of the way I was raised. So I think I see spirituality in things like oceans and mountains and naturally beautiful things. So I hope when you die, you become a part of something like that. Whenever I've had any kind of spiritual experience in my life, it's always been when I've been sitting on a mountaintop or at the ocean or something, so I like to think it will be part of something like that.

"But as far as a conscious life after death, I don't think there's really a conscious life after death.

"I think there is such a thing as a soul, but my idea of a soul is that when it lives on, it sort of...disperses. I don't think my own consciousness of myself lives on, but in some capacity, my soul lives on. I know that sounds weird.

"What I mean is, I think during your life, you're dispersing your soul as you go along–pouring it into people and places and ideas that become so much a part of you that you remain in them after you are gone.

"I know part of me is in my family, and my best friends, and in the first guy I ever really loved, and is poured into lessons that I am especially passionate about teaching, and sits on my favorite rock overlooking the ocean at the end of a secret trail, and at the summit of my favorite after-school hike, and at this waterfall in Cambodia, and on a soccer field in Germany. So many other places and people and ideas that I truly felt myself pouring a part of my heart and soul into. I think that is what remains of me after I die."

Born into a military family in Missouri, Missy credits her parents and their open-minded outlook on life for allowing her to develop her own unique belief system. The family of six moved a lot during her childhood, but they were always a close-knit group. Every Sunday, they took off together for hikes and other adventures, and her mother passed the travel time in the car reading the kids stories from the Bible.

"I love the way, religiously, that I was raised. If I ever have kids, I want to raise them a similar way. My mom is a lot like me, as far as not believing in God in a traditional sense. But she was very big on teaching morality, and she wanted us to be exposed to the Bible, and to learn the same lessons as other people.

"Nature was a big part of my family's life. Every Sunday that I can remember as a child, we went driving—my mom and dad, four kids, and a dog—and my mom read us Bible lessons. So I'm well-versed in the Bible. I know all the stories. We always talked about them as morality lessons, and my mom never said to us whether she thought the things in the Bible were true or not—she just wanted us to be exposed to that. And she kind of left it up to us as we got older, whether we wanted to believe or not. To make our own decisions what we thought or felt about it.

"I have two sisters and a brother, and I think we all wound up thinking differently about it, but I really respect that, because I think it would have been just as easy for her to raise us not saying anything about God or religion. But she didn't want us to not be exposed to something just because it was something she didn't particularly believe in.

"Sporadically through my life, we did go to church. There were times—my mom was a military wife, my dad was an officer—and I think there were times my mom thought it was important to go to church. There were years of my life when we went to church fairly frequently, and there were years, especially as I got older, when we didn't go."

After a short stint at state college in her home state of Missouri, Missy found her way to Alaska, where she graduated from the University of Alaska Anchorage. For the past eight years, she's been spending her days teaching five-year-olds their ABCs, how to cut with scissors, and basic reading skills.

It is a job she truly loves, and along with the necessary academic proficiencies, she tries to pass along some of the same lessons she learned as a young girl. Her parents were both true free spirits, she says, and taught their children to live life with gusto.

"I always look at my parents and try to emulate them," she says. "I have never met anybody in my whole life who has truly lived every moment like my parents. I always say about them—

and it sounds funny but it's so true—that they really have climbed every mountain.

"And I've talked with them about death, and my mom says, 'Don't be sad for me. I've lived an amazing life.' They raised four children, and all four of us are very different from each other, but we all kind of have that same view on life. We go on vacation. We travel and go places and have adventures, so I guess I really just believe in living life to its fullest, and that if something happens afterward, that's going to be a great surprise.

"I guess for me the purpose of life is to enjoy it, and get the most out of it while you can. I just believe that people should try to live with no regrets, so that dying isn't an awful thing. I'm not scared of it; I'm not worried about it. I mean, I think as I continue to get older and it becomes something that is more imminent, I guess that will change. But, no, I'm not worried about it, because of the way I was raised.

"One reason I hesitate to associate myself with organized religion is the idea of being good to please God and get to heaven. I don't like that. I don't like people doing things for an ulterior motive. I want to do the right thing because it pleases me.

"I think people should be able to do that without the idea of a prize at the other end—getting to go to heaven. I care about people, and I feel good about myself when I do things to help other people feel good about themselves, and to me that's enough.

"Even with the five-year-olds that I teach, I don't always want them to want a reward for doing the right thing. I want them to be self-motivated, to feel good about themselves solely for doing the right thing. To feel good about themselves because they helped someone, not because they got a prize for doing it.

"Not that I always do the right thing. I'm not perfect. But I wish people were more like that. To truly do things [just] to make themselves and other people happy. I think that would lead to a more happy, fulfilling life."

Chapter 2:

Jean Francois Fejoz

> *"I'm afraid of being afraid of the great departure. I'll have to be brave. It's hard to go to a totally unknown place."*

Jean Francois Fejoz thinks more and more about death as time goes on. The sixty-five-year-old Frenchman was raised as a Catholic and still retains some of those early beliefs and teachings, but he also eschews a lot of the formal doctrines of organized religions.

"I do believe in God, and I believe in life after death," he says. "At home when I was a kid, we had the evening prayer before we went to bed, all together. I received the education of a standard Catholic boy, going to a Catholic school until the age of eighteen. My belief of life after death might come from that education, and I'm glad of it—it gives hope.

"A life that totally ends after death seems useless and nonsense. My mind cannot imagine a world with living beings who are on Earth just to live and die and that's all. There is no proof, or very little proof, that there are things that happen to the souls once the beings are dead, but in spite of that, there must be something.

"Being christened, God is automatically to me someone who looks like a mix of Jesus and the Holy Father. But when I spend more time on thinking about it, I realize that probably God is someone very different, a Spirit which we won't know unless we're dead. I think that God is the Spirit of which I am a very tiny part. I see the creation and the world, which is the result of it. It is often chaotic and seems nonsense, but not all the time.

"Religions are far from my beliefs now. Religious is when you go to church, pray, and have rituals with others. Religions suppose that some people (like priests) know more than me, although it is very obvious that they are as ignorant (on what it's all about and what happens after death) as me. Their organizations even sometimes lead to violence, wars, etc. So don't consider me as religious.

"I think that when I realized that the priests (teachers or not) could be real bastards, and that the Church was an oppression tool, I realized I should look elsewhere, look at life as it is. I read Voltaire and Rousseau a lot, and I liked their freedom of thought.

"Spiritual is someone who has a deep interest in what is above our will, and nonmaterial purposes. He should meditate regularly and have a behavior in which you see improvements every day. That's not me, either. Let's put that I would like to be spiritual. Someday, maybe, who knows?"

Born in 1949 in Chambery, Savoie, in southeastern France, Fejoz grew up in a family with six brothers and one sister. He is married and lives near Vincennes, just east of Paris. He is the father of three children, holds a political science degree, and has worked for the past fourteen years as a bilingual guide for museums and tours.

In October 2005, Fejoz learned about the famed pilgrimage across northern Spain, the Camino de Santiago, and decided the historic journey undertaken by millions over the past twelve hundred years was something he very much wanted to do. One month earlier, his mother had died, and two months after that, his father passed away.

Instead of traveling to Spain to make his pilgrimage, Fejoz decided to begin across the Pyrenees Mountains in France. He took off from Vezelay, Burgundy in May 2006 and walked through the countryside for nine days. In fall 2007, he picked up where he left off and walked for twenty-one days. He added another twenty-one days' walking in spring 2008, and in summer 2009 completed the pilgrimage by walking another three weeks and arriving at Finisterrae, a small village on the Atlantic Ocean once known as the end of the world.

"In the first years, I did not know what to answer myself on why I walked," Fejoz said of the grueling effort to walk hundreds of miles from the middle of France, across northern Spain, to the Atlantic. "I just wanted to (and that was a good reason enough). Today, apart from the movie that did provide the start, and the unconscious coincidence with my parents' death, I'm sure that my decision came from two primary motivations.

"First, the absurdity of the world that surrounds us, socially and politically (make money and that's all, have power and that's all—in 2006, the president of France was a disastrous and obnoxious person) and the need for me to get out of it, to get away from it. And, also, my own family life was not what I had dreamt of—my two daughters (I also have an elder son) were living the peak of their adolescence, shall I say.

"When I took the decision to try the Camino, I was not aware of the possible connection with my parents' death. The decision was made after having seen the movie (*Saint Jacques la Mecque*, a French film by Coline Serreau). It's mainly in 2009 that I dedicated my walk to meditation on death."

Among the lessons he learned successfully completing the Camino de Santiago was finding an inner strength—both physical and mental—he did not know existed. It was an emotional experience, and one that left a lasting impression.

"The Camino taught me that I was able to do something on a long distance (beforehand, I thought my will was weak). I found that I could make efforts with a result, and my body with two legs only can lead me to the other side of the continent. I realized that, with time, you can achieve real great things. In a nutshell, the Camino is excellent for your ego (mine, at least!).

"I discovered a whole new aspect of life: a passion, a center of interest, with connections in all fields. History, legends, geography, literature, films, associations, religion, and above all, close relationships with the other pilgrims—the future, the present, and the past ones. There are many traces of that pilgrimage in France and in Spain! The Camino is one of the founding elements for Europe. Since my second departure, I've been working to someday get the Way of Saint James waymarked on the ground in the streets of Paris. I write a blog about it; I meet people for it. I made it to get the Pilgrim's Bench and Tree in the north of Paris, and I am now working on the project of an albergue (Camino hostel) for pilgrims in the Paris area."

With plans underway to walk the Camino once again after he retires, Fejoz says he remains unsure about such things as the meaning of life, the purpose for our existence, and why we are here. Since there is no way of knowing what comes next, it is important to make the most of the life we have now, he says.

"We don't know the purpose; our mind is not powerful enough. There must be one, and I suppose we'll know when we die. Knowing that, we have to make our life meaningful. Violence and aggressivity [sic] doesn't lead to good results. We should do our best to be kind to all—make life better for the others and ourselves—but it is very difficult.

"I don't believe in heaven and hell the way they are commonly described. Heaven and hell are inventions by the humans. Heaven and hell happen here on earth: short moments of happiness, quick or long times of despair, suffering, misunderstanding, awkwardness, pain, etc. I believe that after death, there is a kind of peaceful atmosphere. And when we're there, we won't even care about heaven and hell.

"I sometimes pray. I take it as a good kind of meditation exercise or when I need to overtake a difficult time or when I feel I'm in a bad state of mind. It raises my soul. I rediscovered the 'Notre Père (Our Father),' and I realized that the words are very simple, very basic, and could be said by anybody who believes in a superior 'Being.'

"Yes, I'm afraid of being afraid by the great departure. I'm afraid I might suffer a lot before I die. I'm sixty-five, so I think of it more and more. It's hard to go to a totally unknown place.

I'll have to be brave. I don't know, but I believe that our spirit gets mixed with a kind of general Spirit. I think and I hope that then I'll understand what all that (life and death, happiness and suffering, fight and rest, love and hate) is about."

Chapter 3:

Laurie Bryan Larson

> *"To me, it's all a part of the process. There's nothing to be afraid of. There are a lot scarier things in life!"*

Virginia resident Laurie Bryan Larson has experienced a lot of death since being adopted from Seoul, South Korea when she was five years old, but it's not something she fears.

"I feel that we're made up of energy and that is what continues after we die," says Larson, a sixty-two-year-old mother of two grown sons. "Since we're energy, we just reformat back into the Universal caldron of energy until the next go-round, if there is one.

"I'm not afraid to die, but I would like to live a bit longer! To me, it's all a part of the process. There's nothing to be afraid of. There are a lot scarier things in life!"

Larson, who holds a degree in sociology and works in business start-ups and human services programs, says she was put up for adoption when the American man with whom her mother was living gave her an ultimatum: the girl or him. Her adoptive parents had heard through their Methodist church about mixed-race children from the Korean War needing to be adopted, and they could not have children of their own, so they decided to adopt little Laurie.

She came to the United States, growing up in North Dakota and Minnesota, and became very close to her adopted dad, who was blind due to childhood diabetes. Unfortunately, he died four years after the adoption from a long-term illness.

"I never knew my birth father, who was an American serviceman. My birth parents were never married. I'm sure there's a story there, but due to a variety of circumstances, I will most likely never know the rest of the story and have come to the conclusion (that) it's not important. It's the 'what is' of life.

"Although I know that it (giving her up for adoption) was probably one of the most difficult decisions for her (my mom), I feel that she made the decision that was the best for me. If I would have continued to live there, I would have probably been on the streets at a very young age.

"Of course it impacted my life, but I believe it's all a part of my path. It has definitely had an impact on who I am, but it hasn't changed me, because I've always been the person that I am now.

"I would say that my adoptive father's death had the most profound effect on me, as we had developed a close bond in the four years since my adoption, and there hasn't been anybody like him since in my life. He was very sick, but as I mentioned, he was a very open and critical thinker. He attended Boston University Theological Seminary at the same time as Martin Luther King, Jr.

"Everything happens for a reason. We may not know or see it at the time, but I see that my journey has not been random."

Larson was raised in the Methodist church, where her father served as a minister. After he died, the church continued to be an important part of her life but became less of a central focus for her, although she continued to participate, even serving as president of the youth fellowship and attending church camp every summer.

Her now ex-husband was in the US Air Force, and the couple went to chapel on base. She became interested in the Lutheran church—not so much for its teachings, she says, but because they knew and admired the Lutheran chaplain. After leaving the Air Force, the couple helped start a Lutheran church in the town where they lived.

At one time, she also attended a Unity Church, and it was experiences there, along with taking a college religion class, that opened her eyes to other, less traditional possibilities.

"Unity Church was probably where I felt the most comfortable," she says. "I have recently attended a Lutheran church again because the minister was a friend and the people in the congregation were welcoming.

"I'm sure it's been an accumulation of my life experiences that has led me to my beliefs, but one of the most profound experiences that I had was when I was in college and I took a philosophy of Eastern religions class. That was the first class where I actually felt inspired to read beyond the curriculum, and I would say that it assisted in continuing to open my mind to all religions.

"I would say that my personal belief system is probably more closely aligned with the Eastern religions. But I think the bottom line is being the best person that I can be."

Larson says she considers herself more a spiritual than a religious person. She believes in God, but not in the traditional sense.

"I don't feel comfortable with the dogma of religion, but I feel that there are some Universal truths, which are the underpinnings of every religion. I see religion as dividing and spirituality as honoring the whole.

"God, to me, is a life force—the beginning and the end. I believe in a universal life force, and I don't really care what one calls it. I also believe that we each are part of that divine life force.

"I pray often, for others. I believe that there is power in thought. Any hell there is, we either create personally or collectively on Earth.

"I believe that we're each here for a purpose, whatever that may be for each person. Overall, I believe that we're meant to leave the world better in some small way by having lived."

Chapter 4:

Andres Harnisch

> *"I actually look forward to it. I'm kind of interested to see what's coming next."*

Growing up in East Germany behind the famous Berlin Wall, Andres Harnisch never thought much about things like death and dying, heaven and hell, sin and salvation.

In fact, living under Communist rule, it wasn't until he was much older and had moved to the United States that he even learned or seriously considered much of anything about God, religion, or spirituality.

"I grew up in a family where my parents were not at all religious," Harnisch, who was born in October 1977, explains. "They didn't believe in God. I never talked to them about it. It was something that just never came up.

"I grew up without any kind of religion. We were indoctrinated to believe in the Communist Party and our party leaders, and that's how I grew up, so I never really thought about what happens after death and all that stuff.

"People were allowed to practice religion, but those who did certainly had not the same opportunities as the people who were in the Socialist Party. Being a Christian was definitely a detriment to your situation. I don't think they were persecuted, but they were looked on as suspicious. Being religious was suspicious.

"I think the first time that I was exposed to religion—very minorly—was when we had a set of twins in my class in second grade, or third grade or fourth grade, who were Christian. They were kind of talked about by the teachers. The teachers in East Germany—not all of them, but some of them—were very strongly associated with the political party. Those twins were basically looked down upon, and were looked at . . . you know, almost like people who believe in Santa Claus or the Easter bunny. That's kind of how they were treated. It was just something like . . . as if someone had a third nipple. You looked at them like they were a little weird.

"I was friends with them. I hung out with them, more or less. Their father was a baker and worked in the same hotel as my mother. I don't remember ever talking about religion with them."

Harnisch was twelve years old when the wall separating East and West Berlin came down in 1989. He remembers that time as being liberating but chaotic.

"For two or three years after the wall came down, nobody really knew what to do. How do I say this . . . after the wall came down, in the whole of East Germany, everything that was right one day was not right anymore. Things were pretty lawless. A lot of the apartments in Berlin were empty because people fled in '89, and so a lot of the inner city was empty, because people had just left. There were a lot of break-ins and a lot of wild stuff going on.

"At the age of fourteen, we all got wild. I started smoking pot and drinking liquor and partying all the time. We stole a moped from a cop, and the young people—a lot of my friends—stole cars and killed themselves. They were running into trees because the lock on the steering wheel locked in and they would crash.

"By the time I was eighteen, my parents couldn't stand it anymore. I moved out and the less I saw them, the better relationship we had."

Along the way, young Harnisch had also gotten a taste of life outside East Germany, including the United States, through various high school student exchange programs.

The first place he visited, when he was sixteen, was London, and it was a memorable but highly unpleasant experience.

"My first foreign language was Russian. I only learned English in the tenth grade. And my parents knew that English was really important, so they first got me in an exchange program to England, and I hated England. I stayed there with a family who only participated in the program because they needed the money, and so there were like four people crammed into a tiny room. Every day we ate white bread with cheese and ketchup. We had to go to school for six hours, and I didn't speak any English. It was miserable.

"I told my parents I would never go there again."

The next year, he lived with a family in Hagerstown, Maryland, and everything he experienced there was an eye-opener for the young East German.

"When I grew up, we were really raised with the Russian doctrine that basically said, if you Germans ever have power, you will again start killing all the people of the world. So, there was no national pride living in Germany when I grew up.

"The first time I came to the United States, everything was apple pie, baseball, football, family, listening to the national anthem . . . the boy that picked me up drove a '68 Camaro, and the dad has a T-bird, and they took me to baseball games where everyone stood up and put their hand on their heart and sang the national anthem, and I just thought, 'That's what we're missing in Germany.'

"I always said that if the chancellor in Germany had said, 'Germans, we need to all do this for the betterment of the country,' they would have told him to fuck off. Because that's basically what happened in the forty years of East Germany, with the Russians being there and indoctrinating the Germans about how terrible we were and all that.

"So I think national pride is very important, and when I came back (from Hagerstown), I knew that I wanted to live in the United States. From that moment on, everything I did was about being sure to get there."

He was not an outstanding student, Harnisch says, but managed to make it through school, participated in another student exchange program that took him to Hill City, South Dakota, served a year in the military, then returned to the United States and spent a month driving all over the country with an American friend he had met during one of his student exchange visits.

"We spent four weeks driving—I don't know—fifty thousand miles or some ridiculous number. You know when you're at that age, barely twenty, and you love driving? When I started that trip, I *loved* driving—I *loved* the United States. When I was finished, I thought, 'I think I've driven enough for a while.'"

After returning to Germany, he went to work in the hotel business, a job that included extensive training and schooling in all aspects of the hotel industry. All this preparation was paving the way for his big dream of moving to the United States.

"I always wanted to leave Germany. I didn't belong there. I grew up German, and there was certain aspects of German life that I enjoyed, but in general the German mindset is very negative. Our history—the whole Nazi bullshit and all that stuff—is really kind of hanging over everything. I think in the last twenty years, it probably has gotten a lot better."

His first stop along the way, ironically, was back in London, where he worked for two years in the hotel business, primarily so that he could hone his English-speaking skills before tackling life in the United States.

"I knew that I would have only eighteen months' (visa) time in the US, and my English wasn't very good yet. And I knew if I came over to the US without speaking perfect English, I would have no chance to get extended after my eighteen months.

"But London was miserable once again. Really, it is not a great place to be if you don't have a lot of money. I refer to it as a place where you go out once a month to the club and party a little bit, and for the rest of the month, you eat pasta with no sauce.

"I lived in a tiny four-bedroom apartment with one bathroom, with nine people. And most of the money I earned went to rent, so . . . But I learned good English."

After two years and several promotions at the hotel, he applied for a job in the States and wound up working in Dallas, Texas, where he met his future wife, Maureen, a native Texan who had lived and traveled all over the world. After they became a couple, they moved to Hawaii, where the Harnisches now live on top of a mountain overlooking the ocean and operate a business dealing in art, antiques, jewelry, collectibles, and estate sales.

He has come a long way from those days as a hooligan running the streets of Berlin, and that's the primary reason Harnisch says he isn't the least bit concerned about death and dying.

"I look at my life . . . I come from East Germany, (and now) I live on the opposite side of the planet; I accomplished a lot of things that my grandfather wanted to do—he wanted to see the world, wanted to see the United States. I've come from a very rigidly German background that believes that for anything you want to do, you need a piece of paper with a signature, and you have to go to school for three years and come into the system. I can do now whatever I want to, as long as I'm able to produce. No one gives a shit what piece of paper I have or not.

"I'm very happy where I've come so far. If it would be over tomorrow—and don't mistake that for me wanting it to be over—I would be very happy about where I've come from, and where I've ended up.

"I'm not at all worried about dying. I'm really not afraid at all. I actually look forward to it, and not in any kind of morbid way. I'm afraid of suffering, being in pain, and having to lay in bed for a couple of years or something. But I'm absolutely not afraid of dying. I'm kind of interested to see what's coming next."

In the meantime, since he has been in the United States, Harnisch has been exposed to a wide variety of religious beliefs, and he feels most comfortable with the principles associated with Buddhism, including reincarnation.

"It certainly is something that makes more sense to me than anything else. I've met people who had past-life experiences, who had knowledge and interests that had nothing to do with who they are.

"When I moved to Texas and I was exposed to a very strong Christian community, I definitely started thinking that there were some things that didn't make any sense to me. Things like the idea that when a small child dies before it is baptized that it would go to hell, or if you don't believe in Jesus, you can't get into heaven, things like that.

"But Christianity is a relatively young religion. It's only two thousand years old. There are a lot of religions that are much older.

"Then I moved to Honolulu, and I was exposed without knowing it really—because no one ever spoke about religion—to people who just have a certain opinion about life and the afterlife. I think I became much more open spiritually than any other time in my life.

"I started looking at everything in my life—some of the things that I didn't like about myself—and I kind of reinvented myself over here. I thought about my parents and my upbringing . . .

"I've always enjoyed having mentors in my life. I've always enjoyed meeting people with jobs that they really love, and are very passionate and knowledgeable about. In my travels here, I came across someone—a Japanese Hawaiian—who basically shared with me some of his views. I only later on found out that they were kind of Buddhist views. The belief that we basically come to this earthly plane to polish our soul, to learn about life, to be a good person. A good person meaning to do good for others, do things not just for profit.

"You know, if you've ever done something nice for someone without getting anything in return—opened a door or lifted something heavy, something totally unexpected for someone. The pleasure you get out of that is a pleasure that you really don't get out of anything else.

"So over time, there were just little nudges in my life where I kind of started thinking about the idea of us coming back over and over until we have reached a vibration—if you want to talk New Age—that basically allows us to not have to come back to this world.

"I do believe that the world is a place of sorrow. If you look at societies all over the world, there's a lot of pain and suffering and misery. And I look at the afterlife as a place where all the souls basically hang out, and where you get a new job assigned and you come down and you have to go through life. You have to try to vibrate higher by the time you leave than when you came.

"I fully believe that makes more sense to me than what my Communist people said—that you are born and then you die, and that's it. And it also makes more sense for me than the Christian belief. The creator is not like someone with hands and arms, who molds things and forms things and seven days later we have all the planets and all that stuff. To me, that makes very little sense. I look at God more as an energy.

"I don't think about heaven or anything like that. . . I think heaven, or the place where you go after you're dead, is where you don't have any questions anymore.

"I've looked at a lot of religions, and that way of looking at it has helped me become a better person. If you are living every day and trying to do good for other people—without profiting from it—or, if you treat other people the way that you want to be treated, I think there is a certain happiness and a certain way that you live that is much happier."

Chapter 5:

Jennifer Fitzgerald

> *"I've always believed there's a heaven and a hell, and that we'll go to one place or the other."*

Watching her mother struggle with cancer and thinking about the prospect of losing her sooner than later worries Jennifer Fitzgerald a lot more than the question of what happens to her when she dies.

"Mom is like my rock—I just adore her," says Fitzgerald, a forty-six-year-old native of Youngsville, Pennsylvania, population 1,600, where her parents still live. "She's really sick right now. She's had part of her tongue removed, and we're waiting on results to see if it's spread. So I think about her a lot these days. I'll be sad when she goes, but on the other hand, I also think that if it's her time . . .

"She has a great attitude. She's very positive. She says she's had a great life, and I've even interjected, 'You've had some very tough times in your life.' And she says, 'Well, they're stepping stones, and they make me who I am.'

"She grew up very poor, on the wrong side of the tracks; a lot of times they didn't have enough food. But she's still very positive, and I think that's where I got a lot of my positivity—I don't know if that's a word—but I'm a real positive person, and I think I get it from her.

"I think if she were to die today, she'd go to heaven. I know I would miss her, but I can't be selfish, either, because if God calls her, then He wants her. And I know she would never want me to be sad."

Fitzgerald, who became a junior high school English teacher after spending eight years playing trumpet in the US Army, grew up with two sisters in Youngsville, going to Methodist and other churches on Sundays and learning about the Bible. Her parents divorced when she was twelve or thirteen, but that was not a traumatic event for her.

"I was happy about it. They argued so much and fought so much. Sometimes it got physical, and all three of us girls were happy when they got divorced."

Her parents get along a lot better now, and live just a few miles apart. Time has healed old wounds, she says, and once-broken relationships are "great now." After graduating from high school, young Jennifer decided to join the military and see the world. She turned eighteen in basic training.

"I joined for lots of reasons," Fitzgerald says. "One, independence. I didn't want to rely on anyone else to move on with my life. I wanted to figure out what I wanted to do and be. Two, I loved playing my instrument. I played trumpet from fifth grade to twelfth grade, so I wanted to do that, and I did.

"It was a great way to start—like the slogan says. I thought, 'I can get money for college, if I decide to go that route, or I can stay in for a career if I decide to do that.' So it was a good deal all the way around."

Her first duty station was at Fort Drum, New York, and she was stationed for a while in Germany, where she worked a side job slicing meat and cheese in a deli to make extra money so she could travel around Europe, including such places as Austria and Switzerland.

In 1991, she wound up out of the army and living in Texas, where she completed her college career at Tarleton State University in Stephenville. She worked two jobs while she went to school, including tending the shoe department at Walmart and bagging groceries for tips.

"It worked out really good, because you set your own hours. So I'd go to school, go bag groceries until I made enough money for food and gas for the next day, then I'd go home and study, and on the weekends I'd work at Walmart."

Now in her seventeenth year as a school teacher, Fitzgerald, who maintains her musical chops by playing in the Harker Heights, Texas symphonic band, says those early Sunday school lessons have stuck with her, and although her church attendance has been sporadic through the years, her beliefs haven't changed.

"I go through phases. I've been consistent with my beliefs, but I haven't been consistent enough, in my opinion, as far as going to church regularly. I went to church as a kid. When I joined the army, I went off and on. When I got out, there were years when I went, and then I kind of quit going there for a while, and now I go sometimes.

"I do read the Bible regularly, and pray every day. It gives me a good feeling inside, and I truly believe a lot of my prayers have been answered over the years. It just helps me walk with God, and my faith becomes stronger.

"I think the way people are raised has a lot to do with what they believe. I know some people who are atheists and don't believe in God, don't believe in heaven and hell, and I've talked to them out of curiosity, and they grew up that way. I think the way you are raised has a profound influence on what you believe and what you don't.

"I think if you're a believer, and believe in God, and try to do the right things, that you'll be given the gift of eternal life. To me, that means going to heaven. I believe in heaven. I'm not sure exactly what that means, but I know that when I was growing up, we were taught it's a wonderful place where you don't feel pain and you're reunited with loved ones, and that everything's good there.

"I don't have a visual image of God—I don't know what God looks like—but I have the feeling of love and forgiveness and faith when I think of God.

"I think about dying sometimes. I never dwell on it. I just think when it's His time to have me, then it's His time. It could happen in a recliner watching TV, or it could happen in a car crash. I know a lot of people think of death as something detrimental—a serious illness or something traumatic—but to me, you could be gardening or rocking in a recliner and when your number's up, your number's up. It could be when you're ten; it could be when you're seventy, eighty, or ninety.

"It's not really scary for me because there's really no point in wasting time being scared. I have the faith that if I do the right things, I'll go to heaven. So I don't dwell on it or think about it much. I really think more about other people and their salvation than I do about myself.

"It's complicated. It really is. I don't know. I know I don't do everything right. Sometimes a curse word will come out. I like to have a couple of drinks every now and again, but I also know—I always joke about this with my friends—that Jesus turned water to wine.

"I believe in the Bible, but I never quote anything for sure, because I don't know it as well as I should, but . . . there are so many interpretations of the Bible. You could sit here with two people who are churchgoers all their life, and they could argue the same scripture in different ways.

"So, I don't think anyone knows for sure. There's no way of knowing for sure. But I just go by what I've been raised on and what I feel in my heart, and I try to live my life in a positive way. I try to do the right things and be a positive person, and hopefully that will get me there."

Chapter 6:

Alf B. Dahl

> *"For me, it is hard to believe that anything at all happens after we die, but . . . it (also) is difficult to believe that it is all over when I die."*

Celebrating his sixtieth birthday this year, Norwegian marathon runner Alf B. Dahl thinks more about dying than he ever has before, but being in the best shape of his life, he figures he has two or three more decades left before he has to confront that reality.

"I feel very healthy and well, doing a lot of training, eating quality food, my weight is OK, and so forth. Therefore, my own dying is not very much a subject," Dahl says.

"Friends of mine who have died from cancer at a young age have had a profound effect on me. I have become more focused in 'living today,' and not postpone things. This is very important to me, and I try to focus on being mindful in situations that happen and occur. I do not think a lot about my own dying, but I think more about death now than I did before.

"Literally, we become earth first. Our bones last longer, but finally they disappear, as well. This is when buried in the traditional way. If we drown at sea and remain in the sea, we just disappear. Physically. The actual question for me is what happens to the soul after we die. For me, it is hard to believe that anything at all happens after we die, but it [also] is difficult to believe that it is all over when I die."

Dahl, a human resources manager for thirty-five years and a national champion runner in Norway, is constantly in training and runs marathons all over Europe. His personal best time is a 2:54.09 recorded in Berlin, and now he has plans later in the year to run the equivalent of nineteen marathons in nineteen consecutive days, a charity fundraising project he created after completing the five hundred-mile Camino de Santiago pilgrimage in Spain in 2013 with his wife, Anita. When he finally reached the end of the road in the city of Santiago de Compostela after hiking for weeks through the Spanish countryside, he experienced a range of overpowering emotions that led him to want to go back and run the entire length of the historic pilgrimage.

"This sad feeling came over me," Dahl recalls. "I thought, 'It is over.' And I knew I was going to miss the Camino every day in the months to come. To walk all the miles, day after day, eating, sleeping, thinking, meeting people from all over the world, was so fascinating. It made a deep impression on me as the days passed. I wanted to go back. My wife and I had been talking about going back in some years, then the idea suddenly came to me. Can I run the Camino? Is it possible to do it?"

Although he and his two brothers were not raised in a religious home, Dahl considers himself to be somewhat spiritual. He does not believe in God in the traditional sense, nor is he convinced about the existence of a heaven and hell. As a young man, he never even considered the possibility of any kind of life after death, but now that he's growing older, his outlook is slowly changing.

"The question more often occurs in my mind," the father of four explains. "When I was young(er), the question was irrelevant. The question was, so to speak, 'out of the question.' There could not be a life after death. That was the thinking thirty years ago.

"Now, however, thirty years later, I am not so sure anymore. My dad is dead, my mum is growing old, and many of their former friends are dead. Friends of mine have died in cancer, some of them young people. Relatives are dead, some of them in cancer.

"These things have done something to my mind; I do not feel so sure anymore. Is there 'more' than the life I am living now, or is it not? I feel it difficult to believe that it is all over when I die myself one day—maybe in twenty or thirty years. But then the next question is: What life can there be after death? Will my soul exist somewhere else? Will I be able to see those who live? Will I meet those who are dead? I do not know.

"I admit it is difficult to imagine such places as heaven and hell (upstairs and downstairs). Where are they? And is it so that all the good people are gathered in heaven and the evil people are gathered in hell? I find it hard to believe. However, I believe—and really hope—that Mother Theresa and Mahatma Gandhi ended up in another place than Adolf Hitler and Josef Stalin. Therefore, I believe that there must be different places for us. In the real life, it is important to differ between good and evil actions. And that is why I think there must be both heaven and hell."

Growing up, Dahl and his family went to church on Christmas Eve, and for funerals and weddings, but that was it. His home was not a religious or spiritual place, although his grandmother taught him a prayer that he used to recite when he was a boy.

"I still remember that prayer," he says. "I used to pray it when I was small, but no longer growing older. The reason I stopped praying was that it did not seem natural anymore when I grew older.

"I do not believe in God similar to Jesus, literally the father of Jesus. I believe that there is a good power in every human being and that this power is dominating in every person's mind. When I hear or see people pray to God, I think that they trust in the good power. I also think when I hear the word (God), that all people all over the world have something in common: a God to believe in.

"I do not consider myself a religious person, but a spiritual one—yes, I do. This means to me thinking spiritual thoughts and doing spiritual things. For instance, I consider it a spiritual thing running nineteen marathons in nineteen days along the Camino, for the Church Mission in my hometown.

"The meaning of life, in my opinion, is to contribute to others people's welfare. To do nice and good things for your family, your friends, and for your society."

Chapter 7:

Luanne Edwards Gordon

> *"I'll probably have to go and stand before God and look over all the shit that I've done . . ."*

Life hasn't always been easy for Luanne Edwards Gordon, and she is the first to admit that most of the pain she's suffered through the years has been self-inflicted, but after decades of beating her head against a wall, she finally has found peace and direction.

"It took me a long time to get my shit together," Gordon says.

Born in Fort Worth, Texas, Gordon grew up in Houston and graduated from high school in 1975. Much of her life after that was a drug-filled rollercoaster that included multiple trips to rehab centers, but eventually she decided that enough was enough.

"My mother made me go to rehab the first time," Gordon, fifty-seven, says. "I was in my early thirties. She was like, 'You're either going to go voluntarily, or you're going to go to Rusk (State Hospital).' I told her I was an adult and she couldn't do that. But I checked into it and sure enough, she could commit me. So I said, 'OK, I'll go voluntarily.'

"I was sober a good one hundred and twenty days that time, but it took me a lot of rehabs to finally turn my life around—probably four or five."

It was during that initial rehab stay that Gordon first started finding her way back to the God of her childhood. Until the time she was five or six years old, she attended Baptist church regularly with her parents and half-sister, but something happened that caused the family to stop going.

"I don't remember it very much, but we just quit going and never went back. We obviously were very involved in it for a while, because my daddy used to teach Sunday school, but I don't remember much about any of the experience of going to church as a child. I used to pray with my mom before I went to sleep and that kind of stuff, but after that, we never went back to church.

"I found my way back by myself in that first rehab program. It was a biblical-type rehab and I got baptized, but, of course, I backslid—my whole life, I've been backsliding," she says, chuckling softly. "Hey, life's a bitch, man.

"It's funny, because I'd be out by the pool and somebody would come over to me and just start talking to me about Jesus, and I'd be like, 'Man, leave me alone.' It just seemed like God was always pushing, pushing, pushing me towards him, giving me every opportunity to turn to him, but I wasn't listening. It took a long time."

What finally convinced her to turn to God for help in changing her life was an experience she had about five years ago as she was investigating various religions and belief systems.

"You know how I came to be a believer? I guess it was back when we lived in Humble, and I prayed for myself to not be deceived in the end times. Then, I started checking into different things, looking into different beliefs, and I started seeing satanic things going on, and I realized that there . . . my big question was always, 'Why do people just not fulfill biblical prophecy? Why don't they just not have a New World Order? A One World government? Why don't they just not do it?'

"Well, I was so naïve that I didn't realize there are people who have that agenda and believe that Satan is good. What made me really believe in God for sure was that I first believed in Satan. Once I started looking into it, I could see him everywhere.

"I was, like, Satan is real. God is real. And this is just a big ol' freaking holy war. And we're just pawns. That's what I believe."

Nowadays, Gordon is married to her high school sweetheart, works in the deli at an HEB grocery store, and is the proud mother of a son from her first marriage. She hasn't attended church in several years due mostly to her work schedule, but hopes to continue learning and growing in her Christian beliefs.

She follows the teachings of the Bible and believes there are different levels of heaven, which may only be reached by accepting Jesus Christ as one's savior.

"My whole life, I always paid attention only to God. I never really thought that much about Jesus, but the more I learned, the more I realized that the only way to God is through Jesus. I believe all you have to do is believe and you'll get into heaven. I know you have to repent—you have to try, at least—and if you can't, well, you can't. You're human, you know? You were born with sin, so you have to try to repent, and if you can, then good. But if you believe, then I believe you get into heaven.

"I don't think I can really imagine what heaven is going to be like. It's just bright and beautiful . . . I know that there is worship all the time, singing, people are just happy and worshipping the Lord. I think hell is just pretty much a horrible place. I haven't read the whole Bible, but I've read most of it, and I'm working on the rest.

"Hell, I think, is just a horrible, horrible place that no one wants to be. But I feel like I'm going to go to heaven. I'm pretty sure I know what's going to happen. I'm pretty sure I know what I *hope* is going to happen, which is that I'm going to go to heaven.

"I'll probably have to go and stand before God and look over all the shit that I've done, and all the terrible things that I've said, but hopefully he's a merciful God.

"Sometimes I feel like I'm not afraid to die, and then sometimes I feel like I am. Especially since my sister [Iris, sixty-five] just passed, and I'm just wondering what happened with her. I'm not sure if she was a believer or not. It makes me wonder what's going to happen.

"She knew she was dying, but we didn't talk about it. It was a sore subject. She didn't like for me to push her on it, because she had her own beliefs. I talked to her about God sometimes, and I remember one time she said to me, 'You act like I don't believe in God at all.' I don't know, really, what she believed, but I think she's in heaven. I really do. I think, I hope, that she's in heaven.

"Who knows what goes through your head as you are dying? All she had to do was say, 'Jesus, forgive me. I believe in you.' That's all she had to do, you know? Then, she could go to heaven. I believe that deeply in my heart. I believe that when people die and are dying, that is what they think. God automatically comes to their mind. They always call on God. You always call on God when you're dying.

"I believe that's what happened with my mom, too.

"I believe everybody has that last chance."

Chapter 8:

Koi Hatchootucknee

> *"I believe there is a place where the soul goes. The soul never dies."*

Since he was a young boy, psychic medium Koi Hatchootucknee has seen ghosts and spirits, and he has communicated with the souls of hundreds of dead people over the years, so there is no doubt whatsoever in his mind about life after death.

"Oh, definitely, yes," says Hatchootucknee, a fifty-eight-year-old Shreveport, Louisiana native.

"Actually, I don't say there's life after death—I say the soul lives on. I'm not going to say you rise again like Christ and you're walking the Earth. I will say that your soul is what continues to live on. And when you are reborn or reincarnated, I believe that is the same soul that goes with you."

Part Mississippi Choctaw Indian and part Creole, Hatchootucknee grew up with a brother and sister in Shreveport, and has seen and talked to spirits pretty much as far back as he can remember. He mostly kept it to himself for a long time, but there was one adult in the household in whom he was able to confide his unusual ability.

"There were a lot of big graveyards around where we lived, and a lot of old antebellum-type homes around us—big old Southern-type homes that had centuries of different families living in them. So, you know, people were born, people died, there were wakes in the house, that type of thing.

"I'd see spirits as a kid. I had little [spirit] friends that I would play with under the house," Hatchootucknee explains. "We had maids living with us, and there was one maid who knew what I could do, and she prompted me at an early age. I think her talking to me gave me a good understanding of what was going on, because as a child, I didn't know at first.

"She took me aside and said, 'Look, I know that you see your little friend, Billy, and everybody says that's just a thing that kids do, but I know because I'm like you. I can see things, too.'

"She told me, 'What you're seeing is people that have come from Jesus and that's OK. Don't worry about it, and if you don't want to tell anybody, you don't have to tell anybody.'

"So that's what I did for a long time. I just didn't tell anybody, because when you do, people laugh at you and make fun of you, especially other kids. Now that things like that are being better accepted, I decided that I'd better start doing what I was put here to do."

After graduating from high school and then earning an animal science certificate from Scottsdale Community College in Arizona, Hatchootucknee worked "for years and years and years" as an auctioneer for such places as Anheuser Busch, the Houston Livestock Show and Radio, and radio stations, and for individuals like movie stars and athletes. He also has worked as a police officer, paramedic, and deputy sheriff, and in 2000, discovered a talent and love for painting that led him to found Hambone Folk Art.

He did some psychic work along the way but kept that part of his life low-key for a long time, until he began to see a growing popularity and acceptance of such nationally known psychic mediums as John Edward and Sylvia Browne.

"It wasn't until my later years in life that I started doing the readings for people. Once I found out that people like John Edward were on TV, and realizing that people had become more accepting of that, I really went full force with it. I started thinking, 'Well, that's what I do all the time.'

"Before that, I always pretty much kept it to myself. We grew up in the fifties and sixties, and back then you just didn't say a whole lot about talking to spirits. You're either called retarded or put into an insane asylum or something. Back in the past, they burned you at the stake for being a witch, you know?

"What I tell people now—I give speeches to groups and things like that—is that I was given a gift and in order to continue having that gift, I have to honor that gift. If I come in contact with a spirit and they ask me to deliver a message or let someone know something—if you come to me and we do a session together, and a spirit comes through, and I give you the information—all I am doing is repeating the information that they're giving me.

"I meditate about two hours before the session, and then we go in the office, we sit down, and if I can connect with a spirit for them, whatever the message is, I simply relay the message. It's not a two-way conversation like you have on the phone; it's not some kind of voodoo or anything like that. It's strictly me listening and relaying a message to the person in front of me. It's a spiritual thing.

"I tell people whoever comes through, this message is meant for you today. You may want to talk to Uncle Johnny, but Uncle Johnny may not come today. It may be your mother, your grandmother, or somebody who has a specific message for you. You're receiving this message today for a reason. If you don't understand everything, talk to somebody in your family and see what happens.

"I've had people come back a year later and say, 'You know, when I spoke to you, I didn't understand what that meant, but we did find out that I did have an uncle so-and-so, and this or that did happen.'

"They're really blown away, because I sit across from you and I tell you things that in no way, shape, or form I should know. I wasn't in the room with you when you and your wife made this secret, you know? I don't ask you any questions beforehand. I don't say anything to you. I don't get anything but your name. And I tell people, if somebody comes through for you, then it was meant for you. If they don't come through, then it wasn't meant to be.

"It brings comfort to people. It brings joy and happiness to people. It gives them relief to know that there really is life after death. There is . . . like I said, not so much life after death, but there is a place where the soul goes. The soul never dies."

As a medium, his beliefs would seem to be in conflict with his Catholic upbringing. Not true, Hatchootucknee says. In fact, his early religious lessons were excellent training and go hand-in-hand with the work he does now, which includes not only communicating with spirits, but also confronting demons and ridding homes and other places of what he calls "negative energies."

Although he no longer goes to church, he absolutely believes in God, heaven and hell, and everything else he learned as a boy attending services, but through working with spirits and communicating with people from another dimension, he also has come to believe in reincarnation—the idea that people lead many different lives and die many different deaths. He believes the Bible is the word of God, and in fact uses the Bible as one of various tools when he is asked to remove demonic spirits inhabiting someone's home.

"When I was young, growing up very strict Catholic, it helped me because I understood that, yes, there is life after death. We understand at a very early age in the Catholic religion that there is life after death. There are saints. Jesus appeared three times to his disciples after he died and said he was appearing in the spirit form so that they would understand that there is another realm of life.

"When he appeared to them three times after his death, that's what he was telling them. 'This is why I'm appearing to you.' And they were astonished that they could see him.

"So, it's kind of the same thing, what I do.

"I most definitely consider myself religious. You have to be. I know the Bible better than a lot of priests do. If God is not with me when I go in to do these things, I can't do them. I'm not the one who's doing it. It's God, and the power that is vested through me by him. I would never take credit for doing any of it. It's not me. I'm just something that happens to be used to get messages across, or to fight these demons and these energies. If I didn't believe in God, there's no way I could do what I do.

"I grew up knowing that we had saints and angels and things like that, so it wasn't spooky for me to see these things that I really couldn't understand.

"To me, they have crossed over into another realm of life. There is a place where the soul goes. And the soul takes with it everything that was meant for it in the past. What I believe is that you were put here on Earth to accomplish certain things. When you lived your life before this, you picked someone to help you down here, which we call in the spirit world, a spirit guide.

"That spirit guide and you, before you were born again into your next life, sat down somewhere on the other side and made a pact that said: 'I'm going to go through life on Earth again this way, and you need to be with me and help me understand when things happen, why they happen a certain way.' Be it if I'm going to be a cripple, if I'm going to be a rich man, if I'm going to be a poor man, if I'm going to be whatever I'm going to be, spirit guide is always going to be with you and is going to help you.

"Once you have a spirit guide, you come back, you live this life here on Earth—hell on Earth, as they say—and you're put here to learn lessons. You learn so many lessons and then you die. If you were not able to complete the journey or the lessons that you were supposed to learn, what I believe is that when you cross back over . . . let's say, you have a bad temper, you beat your wife, you were just an SOB when you were here, well, when you go back and you cross over, you have to go through school again. You have to go through a learning process.

"When I speak to them, I hear so many of these spirits talk about how they are moving into the next level. 'I have lessons that I am learning,' they say. 'I wish I knew when I was with you what I know now. I could have treated you better and I could have done things differently. But now I'm learning that here.'

"It would be different if I came across something like that every now and then, but when nearly every spirit that you come across says this in their message . . . other than 'I love you,' the thing they say most often is, 'I'm learning things.' So I believe when you pass over, you go to a higher process of learning, and then when you learn that, you go on to another life, and you take those lessons with you.

"I believe you can proceed on to heaven, but I believe there's many lives before you get there."

Spirits, ghosts, and demonic entities are similar in that they exist somewhere else, some other plane or dimension, and they are not visible to most people, but they are vastly different in nature, Hatchootucknee says. And they are all evidence of life after death.

"There's a difference, but people tend to group them all into the same thing, which is why there's so much confusion.

"I'm called by the church here to find demonic entities and remove them from people's homes. Like I said, there's spirits, there's ghosts, there's demonic entities. There's energy everywhere, and how that energy perceives itself is what I deal with.

"There's all these big homes here that have been on the family grounds for thousands of years, and things go on. People move in, and they have no idea of what happened there before. You know, for example, during the Civil War, the basement was used as a morgue.

"So people move into these homes and things start happening, and they don't know why. I'm called to go in and rid the house of that energy—demonic energy or whatever happens to be there.

"If you believe in God, then you have to believe in the devil. Satan was God's right-hand angel. He is a fallen angel. It's the same thing with demonic energy. So, when I go into a house, I have a certain prayer that I use. I have holy water; I have my cross. I have priests go with me, and we go in there, and we corner these guys. They tell us their name, and once the demon surrenders by telling us their name, that is surrendering by the word of God, and they know there is a God, so once they submit to God, they have to leave. That's how you clear the houses of the demonic energies."

One simple and fairly common example of the reality of past lives and reincarnation, according to Hatchootucknee, is the concept of déjà vu, the feeling or sensation that a current place or situation has been experienced before.

"If you've gone somewhere and you thought, 'I've been here in this place. I've never been here before, but I know this place.' That's because, in another life, you were probably at that place. In another life, you were probably part of that place.

"Have you ever met a little kid and you've said, 'Man, that was like talking to my grandfather.' You know, an old soul—you've heard that expression. People who are way more advanced than they should be at their age? There's a reason for that.

"I don't believe in coincidences. I don't believe that you flew all the way to Africa and you can sit there somewhere and tell me that you've been there before. That's not a coincidence. I believe the soul, and the memory of the soul, goes on to live, and carries those memories into the next journey, whatever that is."

Chapter 9:

Suzy Ortiz

> *"A part of me hopes that it just ends. I think eternal life would be rather wearisome."*

Raised in northern Alabama by a Bible-thumping mother and an agnostic father, Suzy Ortiz grew up attending services at the local Church of Christ and being afraid her daddy was going to hell.

"I had a hard time thinking there wasn't going to be a place for my father, because my father was a good person," Ortiz says. "He believed in doing the right thing; he believed in honesty. He just didn't believe he needed religion to give him a moral compass. He believed you should do it because it's the right thing, not because you're afraid of going to hell.

"So, I kind of grew up with the balance, where my mother was a big believer in religion and my father wasn't.

"He just told me that there are all sorts of religions, and they all have some belief that there's an afterlife for people who try to do the right thing. His big beef with religion was that, you know, on your death bed you could kind of confess and accept the Lord as your savior, and then you get to go to heaven. And he goes, 'That's kind of cheating. Shouldn't there but a cut-off?'

"He said, 'I'm not going to be a hypocrite.' "

After graduating from high school and college in Alabama, Ortiz married a West Point graduate and spent the next eleven years moving around the country to various duty stations, including Fort Stewart, Georgia; Fort Knox, Kentucky; Fort Bliss, Texas; and Fort Hood, Texas. The couple eventually divorced, and Ortiz is now remarried with an eleven-year-old daughter. Through the years, Ortiz has slowly moved away from the religious teachings of her childhood.

She still believes in God, but things like life after death, heaven and hell, sin and salvation are concepts she is not so sure about anymore.

"I guess I do believe in life after death, but I don't know if it's because it is just so ingrained in me . . . if it's just what I've always known. But I think over the past couple of years—I'm not questioning God, or maybe I am—I've started thinking about other people and their beliefs in the world.

"I guess I want to believe in it. I want to believe there's something else, and I guess I do believe deep down that there is some guiding force. I don't know if it exactly happens the way the Bible lays it out. I just can't reconcile my image of God as a merciful being not letting all those people in and sending them to hell. I just can't reconcile it in my brain. How do you handle that? There's got to be a better way.

"I think it [the Bible] is a pretty good code for living, but every religion has something very similar. As I've looked at different religions, everybody has something very similar—a higher being who creates, who rewards, who punishes.

"Christians are not that unique. We aren't. Everybody has their own type of prophet. So, is everybody talking about the same person, and it's just their own take on it?

"I always had a hard time reconciling dinosaurs with the Bible. It just drove me crazy. I had a minister sit me down one time, and he said, 'We're not going to discount science. But God created the world in seven days. We don't know how long a day is in God's time. Maybe it's a billion years. So, maybe dinosaurs were there, and then their time was come and gone, and on the second day . . .'

"That kind of made sense to me."

Aside from the experience of traveling around the country for more than a decade, probably the biggest influence on Ortiz's outlook on life and death was her late father, whom she describes as an open-minded freethinker.

"My dad was from Indiana, and he grew up in an entirely different situation than I grew up in. His mother died when he was a young child, he had a father who was an alcoholic, and he bounced around with relatives. He joined the Air Force as soon as he turned eighteen, so he saw the world and he realized there is so much more out there. I think it broadened his horizons. He was very tolerant of other races, other religions.

"He studied other religions . . . he was just interested in the world as a whole. He taught us that you have to keep an open mind. The majority of the world does not believe this way, he said, and you've got to understand and be tolerant.

"My father was very fond of what the Hindus think—that you get reincarnated. He liked the idea of, if you haven't done what you needed to do in this life, you have to do it again and again until you get it right. And the fact that you might come back as something less desirable if you haven't done your best.

"I think he liked that idea of karma. You know, you get what you put into it. I kind of like that idea, too, because I grew up with friends who were Catholic, who would stay out all night and party on Saturday and then go to confession on Sunday. And it was like, but to truly repent, aren't you supposed to not do it again?

"I always felt there were these people who were working the system. In Church of Christ, you have to repent publicly. You have to go down to the front of the church and publicly repent—not real fond of that one. Public confession is humiliating and it's embarrassing. But after awhile, you go, 'Hey, it's the same people,' going up there over and over again."

Like her dad, Ortiz doesn't have much use for organized religion anymore. She considers herself more spiritual than religious but has started thinking about returning to church with her mother, who now lives with her after the death of her father last year from Alzheimer's. She does not want to go back to the denomination of her childhood but thinks she may be able to find something that fits.

"I don't believe organized religion is very conducive to free thinking. I don't believe that blind obedience and faith are the same thing. I think God gave us all free will, and with free will comes the opportunity to make mistakes and screw up.

"A lot of people say they don't believe in God because there are child molesters or there is Ebola or stuff like that, but I believe God gives people free choice, and people are free to make good choices and bad choices.

"I don't know. I don't think I can go back to Church of Christ. I think I have seen too much of the world now that I don't think I can agree with their very narrow beliefs anymore. It's a very intolerant religion. What I remember growing up is there was a whole lot of 'you shouldn't,' and there wasn't a whole lot of the happy part. There was a whole lot of 'don't do this, don't do this, or you're going to hell.'

"I never saw religion as a joyful thing. I saw it as fearful—obedience by fear. I just have a hard time with the idea that there will be so many people who wouldn't be accepted into heaven based on the criteria that most religions have.

"And I see so many people who do so many horrible things in the name of religion and God. Some of the worst atrocities on our planet are committed by religious zealots, and I don't know that I want to be associated with that. I hate all the things that are done in the name of God.

"I was just reading an article on CNN about a former pastor who has become basically agnostic, and he used to think there was no purpose without God, and he said, 'But you should have *more* of a purpose if you don't have a God—because you only get one shot. And if this is all there is, shouldn't you be doing your absolute best instead of hoping you get a second chance in heaven?'

"That kind of resonated with me. I thought, yeah, instead of hedging your bets, shouldn't you be living this life the absolute best you can? Treating it as a one-shot deal?"

Her own death is not something about which Ortiz is overly concerned. She thinks about it sometimes, of course, but believes that instead of worrying about what happens next, it is more important to focus on what happens now.

"I do think about it, and hopefully, there's something more.

"A part of me hopes that it just ends. I think eternal life would be rather wearisome. I really do. Sometimes, it's just hard to get through a day . . . I can't imagine eternity. What would you do without the trials and tribulations you experience on Earth to vary it up a bit?

"I'm deadly serious. I don't know that I would want that.

"Isn't that what makes life meaningful? Knowing that you have a finite amount of time, and you have to make the best of it. If you have all the time in the world, what are you going to do?

"Part of that comes from my grandmother, who was ninety-nine when she died. I remember talking to her once about her hundreth birthday, and she said, 'I never wanted to live this long. I'm tired. I'm old. Been there; done that. You know, at some point, it has to end.'

"Of course, she had outlived her husband, her brothers, her sisters, her parents. She just said, 'It's tiring. The world is changing.' And she didn't live to one hundred.

"I told my mom, 'I don't want to live that long. I don't want to outstay my welcome.' I just can't imagine living forever. I think you have to live your life here.

"I believe in faith. You have to have faith in things, faith in people, faith in humanity. I think you have to have faith that everyone is called to a higher purpose, that you have a calling. I think too often we take for granted that maybe we should be doing more things to help other people, taking care of others, doing our best."

Ortiz, who has a bachelor's degree in finance and economics from the University of North Alabama and a master's degree in education from Baylor University in Texas, worked for a while in banking and then decided to go into public education. Being a school teacher was not her first career choice, but she has been at it now for twenty-two years and thinks maybe that was her calling.

"We [she and her first husband] were in New Orleans, and I went back to school and got a degree in education. My business degree wasn't real . . . transferrable. I worked then in banking, but every time we moved, I had to start all over. We moved around so much that sometimes I couldn't get a job.

"Everybody told me to go back and either get a nursing degree or an education degree. Those are the two best jobs if you're married to someone in the military. I couldn't stand the sight of blood, so I opted for education.

"I taught one year in public school in New Orleans, down in the Ninth Ward. It was rough. We had armed guards in our school. Our parking lot was surrounded by a fence topped with concertina wire. An armed guard would open the gate and let us park in the morning, then lock it behind us. That almost cured me of ever wanting to teach again.

"I don't think I was ever under the illusion that I was going to change the world, but do what I can, while I can. I believe I make a small difference in some kids. Not all kids, but some. And I think that's a good feeling. I don't know how many people can look back and go, 'I affected people's lives.' I think that's a pretty good feeling to have.

"I think if there were a pecking order for heaven, I think teachers would be right up there."

Chapter 10:

Ellory Bockting

> *"I don't know whether I will go on, and I honestly don't consider it to be incredibly important."*

The son of a Blackhawk helicopter test pilot father and Women's Army Corps mother, Ellory Bockting was born in Kentucky and grew up in small-town Indiana, spending a lot of time as a kid "pretty much running around by [himself]" and working assorted jobs as he got older, until he finally joined the army himself at age twenty-three.

Now, the thirty-six-year-old is out of the military, married with one young son, and he thinks about life a lot—almost constantly, in fact. And he loves to talk about his views on life. What he doesn't think much about is death or what happens after that.

"I don't know whether I will go on," Bockting says, "and I honestly don't consider it to be incredibly important.

"Who wants to know that when you die, it's lights-out? But let's suppose that's what it is. You go lights-out every single day, when you go to sleep. You're really not that worried when you're in that lights-out state, and it's not like the world won't go on without you. Every time you go to sleep, or every time you wake up, you're not really thinking about whether the people in France are getting along without you in their lives. So to me, it's a curious question.

"As to what happens after you die, I can't fathom. I've heard lots of claims, but if you look at claims from the objective viewpoint, there's not much you can make of the claims. They're interesting, but you have to be very careful of bias.

"What I have seen people do with religion is typically a logical train wreck. It is a rational disaster beyond belief. One of the first lessons they used to teach in Greece when talking about philosophy was: all humans are mortal, and Socrates was human, therefore Socrates is mortal. So even if I go back to the first philosopher, faith isn't going to prevent you from dying. And the concept of God is so big . . . you're talking about something that created the whole universe. I can't even *understand* the whole universe, but there is something that supposedly created the whole universe and you want me to then have an opinion on what that thing is? It's beyond me. So, if it's true that a deity had done such a thing, it would still be beyond me. How do we even conceptualize it?

"The only thing I can say is that heaven sounds like a nice idea," he says. "But so far, it is only a claim."

Bockting attended church as a kid but eventually grew bored with sitting around listening to sermons that didn't seem to make much sense. He also witnessed a lot of contradiction inside those stained glass walls, and so even as a youngster he went looking for answers at the local library. Throughout his life, in fact, he's done a lot of studying, both in college classrooms and on his own. And he now prefers the theories of philosophy to guide his thinking and beliefs.

"I think that making do with what you have, when you have it, is the whole point of life. Whether I make it or not, whether I survive after my death, or some parts of me survive after death, wouldn't change the rationalization that you only have the facts that you have at the time. And to work with those facts wouldn't change whether you live forever or don't.

"As far as religion goes, what I have seen them do with claiming that morality comes from religion is disappointing. I would have to say that there is not, I think, a right way to live your life. But I do believe that there are certainly wrong ways to do it. And as a result, I am comforted by knowing the right and wrong ways to live my life.

"Knowing that I am not causing harm to other people, and thinking about the fact that my son, Joey, is going to grow up and inherit this world, and what kind of world would I like him to inherit . . . I think this is important.

"It's like saying . . . how often do you ponder whether or not there is life on other planets? Not very often. Is that consequential? Sure, it is. But does it change the fact that you have a life right now, here on this world? People seem to be more concerned instead with going somewhere else. I guess you can call it bad priorities. The world needs a lot of work, and it's sort of like saying, 'I'm going to suffer here long enough, until I'm gone, and when I'm gone I hope my children do better than me.' No, no, no. Focus on the world that they're going to inherit, and then whatever happens to you after that . . . I think that if there is a just God, he would find that to be of value. And if God doesn't find that of value and is more worried about whether you believe this version or that version of some story, I'm not worried about that God.

"I've already achieved a higher moral superiority than that God. If you don't love me, I won't send you to hell, but I'll be darn sure the system is created that way . . . I would never do that to Joey. I would never do that to my son. Not in a million years. So I'm already morally superior—if that's the God that exists.

"The laws of nature seem to be consistent, and that would be inconsistent with love. To me, I would try and find whatever it is that a great superior deity would want me to be . . . being a good person, identifying and learning what is good, and then pursuing that. So often, the pursuit of philosophy is the pursuit of virtue. You ask yourself, like Socrates used to do a long time ago, what is virtue? What is love? And the purpose of philosophy is to try to answer those questions, because those can be easy, off-the-cuff answers if you're not [really] thinking about them. But if you've got a wrong idea about love, a wrong idea about virtue, the damage you do to the world is huge."

So the purpose of life, at least for him, Bockting says, is to be more concerned with the here and now rather than what may or may not come after. To try to cause no harm and to leave the world a better place.

"I would have to say that my purpose in life is to decide for myself who I want to be, and then represent that through my actions. And then, almost like a scientific experiment, observe the effects of my actions.

"If it is positive, [and] if it is good, I want to continue doing that. So the purpose of my life is to see just how far I can take my vision of how I choose to be, from an internal point of view. That, to me, is an achievement. That, to me, is an internal creation. No longer am I going to be programmed by just instinctive programming. No longer do I want myself to be just a subconscious being pretending that's not affecting my conscious choices.

"My purpose would simply be to decide who I wish to be, and then to observe the effects, and then to improve on it. To ask for more than that, it seems, is to be drifting into a realm of subjective wishfulness about what you think the outside world is. Because many people have internal biases and irrationalities that they then project onto the world—because I choose to believe in this, the outside world will represent that. No, the outside world is an objective reality. It is what it is. Just because you feel like chocolate is the best flavor doesn't mean that the outside world has anything to do with that. Chocolate exists, but how you feel about chocolate has nothing to do with it. It doesn't change the nature of chocolate.

"Many people say, 'I have faith [in something].' That doesn't change the nature of what exists out there. It's almost a sense of emotional or pseudo-thinking narcissism to assume that your faith changes the external objective world. To me, if you're going to pretend to be more than what I have already stated, you're pretending that there is something more out there that you're wishing to be true. It is up to you to determine the value of what's out there. It's completely subjective.

"You're determining why you're here by determining what you want to do with what you have. So the 'why' is literally up to you. If someone says, 'Why are we here?' by you determining what you want to do is why you're here. That is the only why you can have.

"Reality is what reality is. It is like looking at a mathematical equation—almost. The real magic comes in your interpretation of what you want to do with it now that you have it. So, 'Why are we here?' is also up to you.

"So, the purpose of life is to determine what you want to do with the information that you have received. Otherwise, you are a determinist who does not believe that you can make a conscious, freewill decision, which I find to be a self-destructive argument, because you're saying, by trying to convince me that I am without choice and without free will, you're trying to convince me to change my actions, which means that I would have the free will to change how I look at the world. So it's a self-destructive argument.

"Why are we here? I would return once again to the argument of: it would be up to you. If it was aliens that made us, well, now that you are aware of this [information], what do you want to do with it?

"You're stuck with a choice. You are always forced to make a choice about what you think of the information that you have received.

"If you don't believe you have a choice, then you've lost free will, or you don't believe in it, which makes the whole point of philosophy moot. It makes the whole point of trying to determine what is the right thing to do moot. It would be like saying . . . Albert Einstein once said—he was a determinist—he said, 'I'm a bit of a determinist, but if someone does something wrong, that person should be punished.' There's a big philosophical whole in that argument. It's not the person's fault if you're a determinist. If you punish someone, you're saying by default that he could have chosen something else. So, if an alien or a god or an ooze came up, it wouldn't change the logical conclusion that you still have to decide what you want to do with that information.

"I had a conversation yesterday with someone who tried to tell me that his particular god is beyond morality. So I said, 'By what standard of morality, then, are you going to judge that your god is good?' He said, 'Well, I cannot possibly judge God because my morality is so bad that I can't determine what is good. So God is good.' Well, I'm back to the question: 'By what standard of morality did you then determine that it's OK to follow this god?' You're forced to think, and you're forced to decide for yourself, no matter how you look at the situation.

"What you do with the information is the determination of the effect that you have on the world. I think that is the 'why?' "

Chapter 11:

Sara Zanini

> *"I think we are going to the heaven, in a perfect place, where we will meet again the people we loved during our life, and we will meet God's love."*

Sara Zanini was raised in Milan, Italy by a very religious grandmother and not-so-religious mother, and her Catholic upbringing and the teachings of her youth remain with her today.

"I used to be a religious person to make my grandmother happy, so I went a lot to the church when I was a child," said Zanini, a thirty-year-old archaeologist. "This helped me getting curious and studying the Bible and questioning about the sense of things. Later on, I grew more aware of some differences between the message of the Gospel and the life of the church.

"I used to go and I still go to the Catholic Church, because I believe it is important to be constant in our relationship with God, and that tradition can be helpful in this direction.

"When I think about God, I think about Jesus and his Father. I pray, because I feel that the relationship with Jesus and with God are like any other relationship in life: if we don't talk to a friend, our friendship will become weaker.

"I think we are going to heaven, in a perfect place, where we will meet again the people we loved during our life, and we will meet God's love. I think we get there as soon as we die: we pass from here to there. I also believe in hell, but I think the hell will be pretty empty. I don't know why.

"I've never thought much about where these places are. I think that the heaven shall be a bit different [for] each one of us, a place where we can be perfectly happy and feel loved, without any need to work, earn money, and buy things. I believe our soul is immortal.

"When I was younger, I saw God in my grandmother's eyes, and love. Later, I experimented [with] his presence in my life, and I felt like I was never alone."

One of the more important influences during her adult life was walking the Camino de Santiago pilgrimage in Spain, a five-hundred-mile trek from one side of the country to the other. The pilgrimage, which translates in English as "The Way of St. James," first began more than twelve hundred years ago when the remains of Jesus's apostle, Saint James the Elder, were believed discovered and entombed in the cathedral at the city of Santiago de Compostela in northwest Spain, near the Atlantic Ocean.

People began walking from all over Spain and beyond to visit the tomb and seek absolution. During medieval times, the Camino was one of the three most important Christian pilgrimages in the world, along with pilgrimages to Jerusalem and to Rome. Millions have walked its pathways since it began in the ninth and tenth centuries.

Today, the Camino has become an increasingly popular destination for not only the religiously minded and spiritually inclined, but also for backpackers, adventurers, and all-around outdoor enthusiasts.

"I walked the Camino de Santiago three times, and on my first trip, I found God," Zanini says. "I already believed that he existed, but I had never felt him in my life. That was the first time I could really feel him, and this feeling really changed my life. That was also the time when I understood that the heart of people is more important than the religion itself.

"I think I am a religious person, but in the last years I'm growing more spiritual, and I feel less attached to religious rituals. I don't think that religion itself can fulfill the relationship with God."

Like most people, Zanini, who is married but has no children, thinks occasionally about her own death. She is not so much afraid of that idea as much as she fears losing loved ones. At this point in her life, no one close to her has ever died.

"Yes, I sometimes think about it. I'm not really afraid of it. I think that if I'm right or wrong and everything will end with our last breath, it's going to happen anyway, so it's not going to be that bad. I'm more afraid about losing other people I love. Nobody who I was really attached to ever died.

"I think that the purpose of life should be happiness and love as much as we can."

Chapter 12:

Brett Sailors

> *"If you're asking if I believe we turn into spirits of some sort and lurk around our old homes and friends, the answer is no, I don't."*

Omaha, Nebraska native Brett Sailors considers himself neither spiritual nor religious, and says during his fifty-six years of life, he has never seen enough convincing proof to cause him to believe in any kind of afterlife.

"As much as I would like to, I don't. I'm a pragmatist at heart and have never seen any credible evidence of any form, or sign, of life after death."

Sailors, who has been married twenty-eight years and has three children, grew up with a brother and a sister in a family that went to services and Sunday school once in a while at a Methodist church. He was never much interested and says nothing has really changed.

"I believe that my parents felt it was their duty to at least expose their children to religion. As with most kids, I didn't like it, as it ate into time I could be playing baseball, football, etc. I never really took to it. My children have had the same type of exposure as me with similar results, to date. They see it as more of an annoyance placed upon them by their mother, who is much more devout.

"I do not consider myself religious nor spiritual in the traditional sense, but I do feel that the old adage 'what goes around comes around' has some foundation in reality. Sometimes it takes too long for 'it' to 'come around' to many people, but I don't believe that one can go around doing bad things their entire life and not expect for some bad things to happen to them at some point. I guess I do subscribe to the notion of karmic justice of a sort.

"My views have been formed over fifty-six years of life. I've seen bad things happen to good people and the reverse. I've seen deeply religious people die too young and the reverse. Going to church does not make a person better, and my experience has been that many people go to church to be seen as churchgoing people. I am not cynical enough to say that I think deeply religious people are fools praying to a little man in the sky who can do them absolutely no good. In fact, I sometimes wish I weren't as cynical as I am and could take more things on faith."

As far as God, heaven and hell, sin and salvation, Sailors basically can take it or leave it all. He considers himself an agnostic and doesn't believe in a judging and punishing celestial father. He believes that when we die, we die, and then it's time for the family to argue over the will.

"They put you in the ground, and your relatives fight over what you left," Sailors says. "I have seen incredibly embarrassing pettiness occur after the death of loved ones. If you're asking if I believe we turn into spirits of some sort and lurk around our old homes and friends, the answer is no, I don't.

"I do not believe that there is some heavenly being watching our every move and rewarding/punishing those who act better or worse. I've worked with too many mega-successful assholes for that theory to hold water. I have also seen too many really good, religious, God-fearing people fail miserably time after time.

"When I think of God, I think of an all-powerful being apparently responsible for the favorable outcome of many major sporting events, as he is thanked often for those achievements. Yet he is never blamed by the loser. Just once I would like to hear someone say, 'We were doing great until Jesus made me fumble on that third down run in the second half!' I mean, I had that [thing] tucked away and suddenly—*bam!*—it's popping out of my hands! Jesus has always hated our team.'

"While I think it is comforting to many to imagine a place of incredible beauty where you're reunited with all your loved ones, with a bitchin', immaculately maintained, Pete Dye golf course on which you could shoot no worse than even par, I believe the concept of heaven and hell that most of us recognize today was shaped centuries ago to help keep the peasant classes from doing bad things to their 'superiors,' rather than use their numbers to rise up and overthrow them. A scare tactic of epic and lasting proportions."

His own death is something Sailors thinks about, particularly since he has experienced the death of both his parents. He is not afraid to die but is acutely aware of the void and sadness that one's death leaves behind.

"The death of my parents had a profound effect on me. The sense of loss is overwhelming. They are the one constant through your life from day one. The thought of not having them around started occurring to me in my twenties, but it still seemed so far enough away that I'd have time to mentally prepare for the inevitability. It was only after they were gone that I realized that there is no amount of time possible to realistically prepare yourself for their deaths.

"I do think about my own dying and am not one bit afraid. Once you die, all of the necessities and struggles of life are satisfied. I actually think people in this day and age live too long, much longer than was intended by nature. Endless surgeries, artificial hips and knees, organ transplants, etc., were never part of the grand plan, as far as I'm concerned. Not saying people shouldn't have or get those things if they choose, but I certainly don't think it's natural."

Despite his beliefs, Sailors, a Sam Houston State University graduate who has worked the past twenty-five years in sales and executive management, says he does attend a Catholic church service on occasion with his wife, who is a regular churchgoer.

The meaning of life for him ultimately comes back down to his self-proclaimed pragmatic nature.

"I believe that the outcome of most situations is typically predetermined by actions taken beforehand. I do not believe that praying for a job offer, a raise, or a loved one's health has any effect on the outcome.

"I believe you should try to do as well as you possibly can, help others along the way if you're able, take care of your offspring by providing them a solid foundation of family and education. To try and instill values in your children so that they can have a life at least as good as mine, if not better, and do the same for their children."

Chapter 13:

Paula J.

> *"I believe our bodies are just that, our bodies, and they will probably just deteriorate—you know, ashes to ashes, dust to dust. I believe that our souls are what will be living in the afterlife."*

Paddling a kayak down a fast-moving river, Paula J. suddenly found herself upside down and trapped under the crush of rushing whitewater. Then, an unseen force saved her life.

"About a year and a half ago, I was kayaking with friends on a very swift and twisting river in Northern Michigan," Paula, who asked that her last name not be used, explains. "I am not new to kayaking—I have several years' experience and mostly on rivers. However, I came around a bend and there was a downed tree.

"Due to the strong current, I could not paddle fast enough to avoid being sucked into the downfall and my kayak flipped. I was under the kayak and able to push myself out, but I could not stand up. I literally 'felt' arms come under me and lift me up out of the water. When I was 'lifted up,' I was standing in about six inches of water!

"I joke about this now but at the time it had a profound effect on me, and I was unable to speak about it without choking up. Now I say that it was probably my mom and dad, and I could hear my dad saying, 'What are we going to do with that kid?' They are my guardian angels."

Now sixty-five, Paula grew up with four sisters and one brother in what she says was not a particularly religious environment, although the family prayed at mealtime and her mother read the Bible. She attended church as a child and converted to Catholicism when she got married.

"My mother had a very strong faith. My father attended church [only] on holidays; however, he believed in God, and in heaven and hell. I went to Sunday school and youth fellowship. It was never emphasized at home, but I think I went mostly because at that age, that is what all of my friends did.

"I became a Catholic before I married my son's father, as he was Catholic and in order to get married in the church, I needed to be one. Interestingly enough, once we were married, he stopped attending Mass. This was a great sadness for me, and a priest told me when I spoke to him about it that I couldn't carry a Bible in one hand and a rolling pin in the other. I didn't quite grasp that at the time, but I do understand now that he was telling me that I was not responsible for my husband's attendance, but for my own.

"Unfortunately, that marriage ended and there I was, a divorced Catholic and not allowed the sacraments. That was when I left formalized religion—but I found my way back. Now, I attend a United Methodist Church—the same denomination I was raised in."

An executive medical and legal secretary for more than forty years, Paula is mother to one child and two stepchildren. She has lived in a number of different parts of the country, including Arizona, Colorado, Michigan, and the Upper Peninsula, which she considers "another state."

She believes quite strongly in things like life after death, the existence of God, and heaven and hell, but there was a time when she had some serious questions.

"Fourteen years ago, one of my sisters died of lung cancer," Paula explained. "My brother-in-law was very angry, because people would send her cards and tell her they were praying for her. He shared his sentiments with me, and I asked him what he thought they were praying for. He didn't know what to say, and so then I told him that I prayed that God would take her home so she wouldn't be ill anymore.

"It was devastating to me to have to watch her be so sick and know that, in the end, she would die. Also, my mother suffered greatly over this loss—she lived with me at the time. A horrible thing, no matter the age, to have to bury a child. Mom never truly got over that loss.

"Then, two and a half years ago, my mother became ill (she was ninety-four years old) and within about eight or nine months, she died with stomach cancer. She was so ill, but had been so full of life for as long as I could remember, that it was a shock to have her so ill. I was her primary caregiver. This was one of the times that I railed at God. Just a couple hours before she died, I went outside and literally begged him to take her home. I asked him why he would make this woman who was the kindest, most gentle and loving mother, a woman who had already suffered great emotional pain in this life, but had always loved him—why would he do this to her? He answered my prayers.

"I was raised with a strong faith, lost my way for a while, and then found my way back. If I didn't believe in life after death, that would mean that all of those that I have loved—many for all of my life—that have left this world, I would never 'see' or 'be with' again. We have been promised something wonderful; I trust and have faith that will be true."

When we die, Paula says, our bodies return to the Earth, reverting to "ashes to ashes, dust to dust," and our souls continue into the afterlife. She believes in the Bible's Holy Trinity, and also in heaven and hell.

Heaven is a wonderful place where there is no sickness, no pain, no sorrow, while hell will be just the opposite, according to her.

"I believe we get to hell by not trying our best to follow God. We are not meant to be perfect—no human is, and that is not how God planned it. He gave us free will. I believe that he hoped we would try and make the 'right' choices. Follow the Ten

Commandments, take care of those less fortunate, be kind, and love one another. I have always thought that unkind people and people that turn their backs on those in need were probably purchasing a one-way ticket in the opposite direction of heaven!

"However, I was taught that God is a loving and forgiving being. He *wants* us to be in heaven with him—and if we are truly sorry for our sins, we will be forgiven. My dad used to tell me that I couldn't go do what I wanted, knowing it was absolutely the wrong thing to do, and then say, 'Oh, sorry about that,' and expect that it would be all OK. But that if I did something that I knew was wrong, and then was truly and totally remorseful for that and asked for forgiveness, then God would forgive, but it's not a 'dicker and deal' type of thing. This has helped me more times than not!

"I am not sure if we will 'see' our loved ones so much as recognize their presence. I have that experience in this life often—where I know in my heart of hearts and can sense that someone that has passed is 'with me.'

"My mother, who was a woman of faith and seriously should have been a candidate for sainthood, used to say she thought our 'hell' was here on Earth, and that we paid for our sins in our daily lives. Interesting thought . . . but just the same, I believe we will pay for our sins, but that in the end God loves us and if we truly love him and trust in him, that we will be in heaven in the afterlife. With that thought, then perhaps the only ones that will be in hell will be the ones who 'denied' God. Scary thought, as my son believes in a 'higher being,' but not necessarily God. I keep apologizing to God for this, as I feel I must be partly responsible for that belief—or I could blame one of his college professors!

"I believe in God, but that does not mean that I don't question when bad things happen to good people. I have told many people, 'I'd rather believe and maybe be wrong, than not believe and maybe be wrong.' Think of the consequences . . . I'd rather be a believer.

"Seriously, though, I'm not sure, other than I seem to be convinced and I believe what the Bible tells us, knowing that twelve people can read the same passage and come up with several—perhaps twelve—different interpretations. I have questioned God many times and even questioned if he truly exists. I have loved ones that have had horrible things happen to them and have railed at God and asked, 'Why?' I still come back to believing that those things are not the work of God, but of Satan, and I still don't know why, but perhaps nothing more than it is more comforting to think that evil is done by evil."

Because of all these beliefs, her own dying is something she thinks about but does not fear, Paula says. She is not ready to go just yet, but when the time comes, she is convinced she knows what comes next.

"I have had three near-death experiences in my life (and I am a healthy person). All of these experiences have strengthened my faith. I know that prayers are answered. I am not afraid of dying. I do, however, realize and know that I don't get to choose when that will be. I am not afraid because I have been told he is preparing a great place for me and I believe that!

"I raised my son; I have two wonderful grandsons. They were my 'purpose' for many years. My purpose now has turned more to helping the needy—working with my church family to help our community and those less fortunate that live here.

"I am a religious person/spiritual person—not to be confused or known as a religious zealot. I pray because it is how I communicate with God. I am thankful for the life I have and for the opportunities I have been given. I also am thankful for the struggles that have been, as they have made me stronger and who I am today. I have instances of prayers answered (within minutes of asking), so I know he is listening.

"As I stated earlier, I wandered off the path for many years and then it was as if a switch was flipped and I realized that I needed, and also wanted, to return to church and God and to put my trust and faith in him. Why? I enjoy being with like-minded people and participation in ministries (choir, missions, etc.). To me, this means that I will spend eternity with God in heaven."

Chapter 14:

Robert Forrester

> *"If, in this life, we are successful in our sincere quest for God-consciousness, we stand a chance of returning to him in heaven, or at the least to a new life where we can continue our spiritual path."*

Becoming a caregiver for his increasingly frail ex-father-in-law was an important part of his ongoing journey of self-fulfillment and enlightenment, and helped convince British entrepreneur Robert Forrester that he is on the right path.

"It was something I did for several months because I was free and the only person who could," said Forrester, a sixty-three-year-old native of Bexhill, Sussex, United Kingdom. "He was isolated and alone in his apartment, and confined to permanent use of oxygen, either connected by hose to an oxygen-concentrator or from portable tanks.

"He had trouble walking, and I became his ticket and help to the outside. Regularly, I bundled him into his chair, grabbed four hours of oxygen, helped him into the car, and drove him around. We would visit the doctor, the hospital, the lawyer, stores, the bank. Each place, I would help him in and out and make sure we didn't forget to return before the oxygen ran out. We often went to the diner together.

"One day, we were out driving . . . he was this generous, spiritual-but-not-practicing, old Jewish guy. His name was Lou, and we had known each other close to thirty-five years. Honestly, during most of that time, my attitude to him was not always that generous . . . complicated. Anyway, he turns to me and says, 'Robert, I have a confession to make.'

"I was struck dumb and had no idea how to react. But eventually, I asked him what he meant by a confession. He turned to me again and said, 'Robert, I love you.' I was dumbfounded. No man—my father certainly never—had ever said those words to me. It was a huge, huge gift to me, one that certainly and permanently changed how I am with my own two sons, and increasingly more with people in general since. Shackles and scales fell!

"Three days later, Lou had passed away. His simple words were a gift from God. 'I love you, too, Lou.'"

For most of his life, Forrester held "some vague belief" in a higher power, and attended the Church of England (Episcopalian) throughout his youth. Educated in a boarding school from the ages of nine to eighteen, chapel attendance for young Forrester was compulsory every Sunday. None of this had any positive effect, other than fostering an appreciation of organ music, he says.

After age nineteen, he never "willingly" stepped foot inside a church again, although after marrying a Jewish woman, he attended synagogue frequently during the next thirty years. That exposure to Judaism is part of the foundation for his somewhat unusual and eclectic belief system today.

"My best way to God, I trust, is through the words of Jesus," Forrester explained. "I am a follower of his. My children (two boys) are Jewish. I believe this is a part of God's plan. Were I not exposed to the Jewish faith, which I have to admit is quite foreign to me, I feel I would be some intolerant ass. But faced by rejection by my fellow Christians of the Jewish faith, I had to take stock.

"My sons are Jewish! Would an all-loving God reject them and all the Jews—and, by extension, most of the rest of the world's population whose faith tradition is not Christian? No way. I know an all-loving God, [and] the God I believe and trust in would not provide only one way back to him. I am sure that all faith traditions are gifts from God and ways to extend his light, love, forgiveness to all peoples on Earth. How could it be any other way?"

A turning point in his life came four years ago when Forrester discovered the Camino de Santiago pilgrimage in Spain, and that journey led to an ongoing discovery that not only brought him closer to God than he has ever been, but also to the knowledge and belief in such things as reincarnation. He can just as easily cite the Bhagavad Gita (Hindu scriptures) as he can the Bible.

"I'm not an expert, but [I believe] another path available back to God is found in Hinduism.

"Hindus believe the self or soul (atman) repeatedly takes on a physical body. According to the Hindu sage, Adi Shankaracharya, the world—as we ordinarily understand it—is like a dream: fleeting and illusory. To be trapped in samsara (the cycle of birth and death) is a result of ignorance of the true nature of our existence. It is ignorance (avidya) of one's true self that leads to ego-consciousness, grounding one in desire and a perpetual chain of reincarnation. The idea is intricately linked to action (karma), a concept first recorded in the Upanishads. Every action has a reaction, and the force determines one's next incarnation.

"The Bhagavad Gita states: 'Never was there a time when I did not exist, nor you, nor all these kings; nor in the future shall any of us cease to be. As the embodied soul continuously passes, in this body, from childhood to youth to old age, the soul similarly passes into another body at death. A sober person is not bewildered by such a change' (2:12–13). 'Worn-out garments are shed by the body; Worn-out bodies are shed by the dweller within the body. New bodies are donned by the dweller, like garments.' (2:22)[94]

"This is a concept I do not find particularly at odds with the words of Jesus.

"At this stage of my life, the 'ravages of age' are for sure now quite obvious and undeniable," Forrester says. "I am still in pretty good health and treat myself properly; few people think I am my physical age. However, I now know and embrace who I really am—namely a never-changing, eternal spirit temporarily animating and navigating this physical, ever-changing body.

"We are here with the free will to want to love God or not, or even recognize his existence. Should we do so and express a sincere desire to return to God, he will be overjoyed and begin helping us. Since I am not my body but eternal spirit, I know death of the body is not the end and so have no concern about dying. The only concern I would have is for my loved ones and how they may feel."

He does not attend church, due in part to both time and distance, Forrester says. His church is one and a half hours from where he lives, and he also cares full-time for his mother. His faith is strong, however, and he does not feel the need for religious ritual.

"My path has led to me to the point where I think of God often during the day, praise his holy names, see his works in everything, and trust he is there for me. Stuff happens on a regular basis to confirm and support this belief and trust.

"We are here in this physical realm because we became selfish and self-centered—in essence, we wanted to be like God. Being the all-loving God he is, he obliged us [by] creating and placing us in this physical universe free (love exists only if one has free will) to live a life away from him and work at being 'little gods.' Always in the hope, on his part, that we would eventually recognize our weakness, realize our true essence as 'loving servants,' and want to return from this hell (this is it; we are already in hell), and resume our natural state in the spiritual world, loving him for eternity.

"So, if in this life we are successful in our sincere quest for God-consciousness, we stand a chance of returning to him in heaven, or at the least to a new life where we can continue our spiritual path, albeit still in hell. Or, if we live lives of selfishness, without God, depending on what we have done with this life, so we will reap the consequences by being returned to a life of lowered human circumstances, or even less capable forms of life.

"In the meantime, daily I endeavor—frequently failing—to be a better, more loving person, to find my way back to being a loving servant of God. One thing I believe, though, is through my thoughts and actions, I come to know the true meaning of Jesus's words: 'The kingdom of heaven is near.' Near, so I get the occasional glimpses of it; it is a spatial and not a temporal reference meaning, 'it's right here and we can experience it now.' It's not some far-off time of the second coming. Also, Judgment Day for me comes at the death of my physical body and, as reported in thousands and thousands of near-death experiences, my spirit will take the tunnel journey toward the ineffable light portal of heaven, where there and then, judgment will be rendered."

Chapter 15:

Amber Iversen

> *"Nobody lives forever, so it's not something to be afraid of. You can't live your whole life fearing something that is inevitable."*

Arizona native Amber Iversen is not afraid of dying, but she thinks about it quite a bit, especially for some reason when she gets behind the wheel of her car.

"It's funny, but a lot of the time when I'm driving, I imagine driving off the freeway or smashing into a tree or something," the twenty-five-year-old bartender and photography student says. "I don't know why, but when I'm driving, I always think I'm going to get into a car wreck and die. I think about it way more often than I think I should . . . it's really weird.

"Sometimes I wonder, I guess, when I'm going to die or how I'm going to die. But mostly, I don't think about it much. It's really only when I'm driving.

"I don't think that I am afraid. I can't really explain it. I know that whatever happens when I'm gone, it'll be OK. My family will be sad, and that sucks. But everyone is going to die eventually. Nobody lives forever, so it's not something to be afraid of. You can't live your whole life fearing something that is inevitable."

Iversen grew up in the Grand Canyon State with an older brother and lots of cousins and other family members. She was not raised in a religious environment but enjoyed long discussions about spirituality with her grandmother, who remains one of the biggest influences on her beliefs.

"Most of my family went to church, but I never really did. My dad wasn't that religious . . . my mom is Catholic, so she wanted me to go to church, but my dad never went, and he gave us the option. I've been a couple of times but never really liked it.

"I wasn't raised religiously, but I've always believed there is a higher power. I wouldn't say God, as what everybody else in today's religions believe—that there is one superior being. I believe in a higher power; I just don't believe in God and Jesus and the Bible and everything, especially since the Bible was written by man.

"Most of my family believed in God, but I don't know . . . I just never felt that way. I always felt like I had a different spirit animal—like I was an eagle, you know? I didn't think there was a God that just made me to stay here, and then I go to heaven and I'm still me.

"And hell—I don't think there's a place where your soul doesn't balance out, and you're on the losing end of that. You go to hell and are burned and ripped apart over and over for eternity. I don't think anybody deserves that. This inconceivable horror . . . I don't think that's an actual thing."

For a long time, Iversen has believed in reincarnation, something along the lines of Buddhist principles. Part of that comes from her grandmother, and part of it was just always there, she says.

"I would say my beliefs are along those lines, definitely. I do feel that we are here for a purpose. I think the purpose is just to find happiness. I know that's really basic, but I don't think it's to become wealthy or famous or anything like that. I think it's just to be genuinely happy with yourself.

"I just think that our souls don't just live this life and then stop. I feel like it's a never-ending cycle of energy. I think our spirit gets reincarnated, and you take on the life form of something else. Maybe it could be a tree, a dog, a beetle . . . I don't know. I feel like it's something else, or maybe we could even be another person. You know how people talk about having past lives? I feel like that could happen, too. I just believe in the recycling of energy, basically.

"I don't really know where my beliefs come from. I guess I could say my grandmother. I remember when I was little, we were always getting into these really in-depth conversations, and she kind of asked me what I thought about these things.

"She's really the only one I connected with on that level. My dad wasn't religious or even spiritual, for that matter, and my mom just wanted me to believe in God—and I didn't—and she wanted me to go to church, and I wouldn't, so we just stopped talking about that altogether."

Iversen, who now lives in the Austin, Texas area, was close to her grandmother during that time and even went to live with her after her parents divorced and her mother remarried.

"He was a terrible person, and I'm pretty sure he was insane," she said of her stepfather. As she entered her high school years, the relationship with grandma soured.

"When I was little, we had a really good relationship, but when I got a little older, and I started going out and partying and stuff like that, she didn't like that too well. She actually sent me to go live with my dad after that.

"She's not super strict, but she didn't like what I was doing. She didn't drink and didn't like alcohol, so she didn't approve at all of what I had started doing.

"I don't talk to her that often because she's back home in Arizona. We'll talk on Facebook every now and then, just because it's convenient, or we'll text each other maybe every other month or so. You know, 'I love you' messages, that kind of thing.

"But when I go visit and I see her in person, it's completely different. It's like nothing ever happened. So I guess we have a good relationship."

She hasn't experienced many people close to her dying, Iversen says, but there was a boy she loved who unexpectedly passed away, and his death still affects her.

"The first boyfriend I had, we dated for three years, and we had a really bad falling out. And he passed away last year. That was really hard for me, because he tried to call and apologize and I wouldn't accept his apology. Then he passed away.

"I felt really bad, never accepting his apology. That's definitely a life lesson that I learned the hard way. You have to forgive and forget—especially if the person is willing to apologize."

A former marine biology student at Texas A&M University at Galveston, Iversen says spirituality continues to be an important part of her life as she works to complete her final year and a half of photography education. She is not much for prayer or meditation but is interested perhaps in yoga as a way "to help [her] find more peace and relaxation in [her] life."

Someday, she might even step inside a church.

"I would say I'm definitely more spiritual than religious. It's hard to say that I would be religious, because I really don't have a religion. I probably should do some more research, because I'm sure there's one out there that fits me, but I don't want to define myself in one category and then find that I don't agree with something in that religion. I don't think there's one strict religion that I could follow 100 percent, all the way.

"I think it (spirituality) has a big part in my life, even though I may not realize it so much. Growing up, my grandma definitely had a big part in that. She is very spiritual. She believes in . . . gosh, I can't even really explain it. She's really old-fashioned, and she's all about zodiac signs and essential oils and natural healing, all these things. She's a very complicated woman. Very spiritual, but not religious.

"I think that I have an old soul, I suppose. I always felt that way when I was growing up. I never felt naïve . . . I felt like I was more advanced than other kids my age, in everything, really. I really don't know why I believe the way I believe—it's just something I felt inside, and I can't really change it. I still feel the same way I did when I was six years old."

Chapter 16:

Swami Yogeshwaranand Bharti

> *"Life after death . . . is not myth or mysticism, but a real fact."*

Heaven and hell are places that absolutely exist, but not as some mysterious final destinations for people after they die, according to Swami Yogeshwaranand Bharti, a forty-two-year-old monk in Hardwar, Uttarakhand, India.

Instead, both places are right here on Earth.

"Yes, I believe in heaven and hell," Bharti says. "They are not elsewhere. They are on this Earth we are living on. We get good and bad, as reaction of our action in future, in this or next birth, under the arrangements of God to filter us. All kind of goodness is heaven, and bad situations are hell, as fruit of our actions.

"Every action has a reaction, if it is done with the thought of fruit in return. This thought is the reason of pains at large. Thought concerned to fruit is boundation, for which one would have to take (another) birth, and would receive good or bad fruit in the next birth. The kind of next birth depends on God, as he knows how to filter us by prize or punishment. One takes birth according to the entanglement of mind at the last time, in the last birth."

Bharti, who calls himself a spiritual practitioner and preacher, graduated with a degree in commerce from the University of Delhi in India, where Hinduism—the world's oldest religion—is the dominant faith. Indian children are taught from a young age to believe in God. About 80 percent of India's population is Hindu, and thirty million more live outside India. There are approximately nine hundred million Hindus worldwide, making it the third largest religion, behind Christianity and Islam.

Basic Hindu beliefs include five basic tenets:

1. The existence of a supreme being and creator.
2. The universe undergoes endless cycles of creation, preservation, and dissolution.
3. Individuals create their own destiny under the cause-and-effect laws of karma (what goes around, comes around).
4. Reincarnation of the immortal soul, which evolves through many births and lives.
5. No particular religion teaches the only way to salvation.

"I believe in God, yes," Bharti explained. "I think one should always believe in some power keeping each and every thing under control. Otherwise, we have the mentality to fight like animals. Also, every scientist is just doing plus and minus in what God has offered us. Scientists cannot create anything on their own. It is God's grace helping us and giving due credit to we people.

"I pray to God as I am not the real doer of all actions in reality. Because it is God's power as prana (breath) and soul to make me to do all activities.

"We people in India do not think it strange to listen to the word 'God,' as God is in our culture, in our breath. From the very period of understanding in childhood, we are guided about God from parental series.

"We Indians get spirituality from culture through parental series. Finally, it depends on you to go ahead deeply or not, to understand truth of life, to have real and eternal peace at mind.

"Being religious does not mean to go to temples or churches. Spirituality is concerned with the mind, to make one real human being full of real love, peace, and happiness in every situation, with due attachments in God as truth only.

"The purpose of life is to meet and merge in God, as there is nothing [else] to give eternal satisfaction and peace. Do each and every action without thought of return, and offer action and its fruit to God as the way to liberation—because thought of [getting something in] return is boundation. Real meaning of living is to keep aware, yourself and others, about reality of this mortal world and the immortality of God.

"[Too many people] are living like sheep, following each other, and resultingly getting periodic pains and unhappiness, without thought of getting stable happiness and peace—and meaningful life and its end, too.

"One should always remember death, as it must happen. Each and every death affects me a lot and teaches me to get prepared before, as it is inevitable and the way to get a new body, or liberation from the rebirth circle, too. One takes birth according to the entanglement of mind at the last time, in the last birth. I always have thoughts of [being] prepared [for] death. I am not afraid of it. Life after death . . . is not myth or mysticism, but a real fact."

Chapter 17:

Brooke Lewis

> *"There's just no way I could not believe in guardian angels and life after death. It's been right there, in my life."*

Two years after her grandfather died, Brooke Lewis says she saw him walk down the hallway of his house with a newspaper in hand and sit in his favorite chair. Just as quickly, he was gone again.

"He died when I was thirteen, my mom's dad," says Lewis, who was born and raised in northwest Ohio. "We were very, very close. He had four grandkids, and I was the only granddaughter. Perfect [and] could do no wrong. Once a week minimum, we were out there. Family day—cousins, grandma, grandpa. Every birthday, every holiday, all my dance recitals, softball games.

"It was cancer, and it happened really fast. It was really rough. Nobody expected it.

"A couple of years later, I was cleaning my grandma's house. She really couldn't do any cleaning. I was mopping her floors, and I had music on really loud, just jammin' and having fun. Then for some reason, I just felt like I should turn off the music.

"So I turned it off, and I go back to cleaning the floors. They have one of those old door bells with the long metal chimes, and the chime went off. I looked up and I could see the chimes swinging . . . but they're not connected. My heart jumped. I thought, 'Oh my gosh, why are those moving?'

"I ran to the front door and looked, and there's no one there. I could see those things were not connected, and I looked up and saw my grandpa walk down the hall into the living room. He was holding a newspaper, and he sat in his chair and rocked. It looked like him in real life, but just not . . . solid. I don't know how to describe it. He walked normal, not floating or anything. And then I couldn't see him anymore, and I just stood there and watched the chair still rocking. Then it stopped.

"I started crying, and I called my mom. She said, 'It's OK. I've seen him there.' I said, 'When did you see him?' She told me she had seen him several times. Later on, I told my brother, and he said, 'I saw him, too. I was cutting the grass, and he was standing there in the window, watching.' My cousin, the exact same story. I just think he wasn't ready to let go of any of us, so he just kept watching over us until we grew up and got older.

"I always felt very safe in that house. And it's not in the best neighborhood. My mom and I have talked about how when she's sad sometimes, she'll just go there and sit on the couch. She says, 'I just feel safe; I feel like the house is protected.'

"All four grandkids have lived in that house at one point, and little things will happen. In the middle of the night, the blanket will get flipped up and someone will start pulling on your toes. Grandpa used to do that. When I was there, he never messed with my toes, but sometimes I'd hear somebody upstairs. He slept upstairs and my grandma slept downstairs—they'd been married for fifty years and they were kind of tired of each other, so they slept in separate rooms—and you'd hear him walking upstairs sometimes. You'd hear him whistling. And when I'd get scared, I'd always say, 'Grandpa, if you're messing with me, you need to stop.' And he would stop.

"This was just a year ago. When my husband (a US Army pilot) was deployed, I went back home. I think after I was the last one to live there—I was there from July to September (2013), and then November, December, and January—then he decided it was OK to move on."

Lewis, thirty-three, graduated from Lourdes University near Toledo in 2003 with a degree in middle education. Soon after, she married Nathan, a native of Kansas who was also attending college in the area and worked with her at a Dillard's department store. After he joined the military, the couple began traveling all over the country, including assignments in Ohio, Alabama, Georgia, Arizona, Texas, Washington, DC, and Virginia.

During the past twelve years, Lewis has earned a master's degree from George Mason University in Virginia and taught public school for a total of seven years. Teaching was not her first career choice, however.

"I actually wanted to be a Radio City Rockette, but I was too short. This was a real deal. They were auditioning in Toledo, and I was all ready to try out, but I found out right before auditions that I was too short. It was horrible.

"I also considered going into the Air Force and trying to get into NASA to become an astronaut—I'm really good at math and science. But the Air Force recruiter said, 'Sweetie, with your back and your eyes, you're never going to fly a dang thing.'

"But teaching was always one of those things I enjoyed doing. I played school as a kid. I taught dance, and I was a cheerleading coach for little kids. So I was always kind of teaching someone something anyway, so it wasn't too far off from the stuff I enjoyed doing."

Growing up, Lewis attended a Catholic church and still considers herself a Catholic, although her views have changed as she's gotten a little older. She believes in God and in heaven, but the idea of anyone having to spend eternity in hell bothers her quite a bit.

She thinks that no single religion has the answer to how a person earns the right to go to heaven, and she thinks there is more to it than simply believing in a certain set of prescribed rules and regulations.

"I don't think it has anything to do with religion. I consider myself a Catholic—maybe not such a good Catholic—but I don't think it matters what religion you choose, as long as you choose a morally just life. As long as you believe in not hurting others. Now, if I had someone tell me they don't believe in God, would I debate with them? Yes. I would say, 'You're crazy—how can you not see this?'

"I feel sorry for them, but I don't think they're going to be sent straight to hell because they think wrong. As long as they are living a morally just life where they try to do good, try to leave the world better than you found it, not doing anything intentional to hurt anyone . . . I can't bring myself to accept that one religion is the only way to go. I think it's one of those things where you should find what fits your beliefs best and go with it from there. They all have the same basic principles. Even the non-Christian religions have a lot of Christian tenets, if you really study them.

"I think what matters more is how you treat the world; how you treat other people.

"Hell is something I actually go back and forth on. There are some people I think must go straight to hell. But then I wonder . . . there are some people who seem like they should go straight to hell, but maybe there is just something really wrong with them. And I think, 'How could a forgiving God be so cruel to some people?' It's a struggle. But I do have a firm belief in heaven. It is there, and that is where we go."

Along with the vision of her grandfather, Lewis has experienced visits from other spirits, as well. So have other members of her family. Nobody is crazy, she says, but instead may be more in tune with such things as spirituality and the afterlife than other people, due to their Native American heritage.

"I think part of it has to do with the fact that, number one, I'm a pretty perceptive person. I pick up on a lot of emotions from people that they're not wanting people to know about. I pick up on little weird things, sometimes way before people even realize it themselves.

"I just think I'm emotionally perceptive, and I'm open and believe in it. I think if you don't believe in anything like that, you're not going to see it. It's not that I go looking for my grandpa, but I miss him, and I believe he is still watching over me, so I think it opens the opportunity. You have to believe in something in order to see it.

"And I think it has something to do with my Native American background. Just culturally and spiritually, they were very open to it, always trying to find those signs. I think that's why my step-grandpa, I've only seen in dreams."

After the death of her grandfather, Lewis's step-grandpa died suddenly after a cancer diagnosis when she was fifteen. She was devastated and has recurring dreams about him that are extremely lifelike.

"I don't dream about him often, but when I do, it's usually one of two recurring dreams. In the first one, we'll be in some kind of room, and there's almost like hospital beds, and we'll be talking and hugging, and saying I miss you and I love you, and just kind of catching up.

"Then, he always leaves. And when he leaves, he goes through a door. The door has almost like a doggy door in the middle, and I look through it, and on the other side is a playground. If you know me, I love playgrounds. I love swings. And the sky is just always beautifully lit up with clouds, and the sun is streaming through, and you can see the rays. It's so pretty. And you can see people. Not even faces, but just people playing and having fun.

"And I keep saying, 'I want to come.' And he gets really adamant, and says, 'No. You can't come right now. It's not your time. You don't belong here. I'm still watching over you.' And then I wake up.

"And there's another one: I'm in this place, and it's a multi-level . . . it looks like somewhere you'd go and play laser tag. And I have my grandpa with me, and we're looking for my husband, Nathan. I keep saying, 'I want to find Nathan; I want to find Nathan. I want you to meet him, because you'd love him so much.'

"And my grandpa always says, 'I already met him. I watch over him all the time.' My husband is a pilot, and he has been on five (overseas) deployments, and sometimes I wonder if he is going to come home. He's been near some really bad stuff.

"So there's just no way I could not believe in life after death. It's been right there, in my life. I really feel there are guardian angels hanging around. I think they're just not quite ready to move on. For some reason, they're staying on, and there are people watching out for me; keeping me safe. I think that we've taken the words 'ghosts' and 'angels' and all that, and turned them into stuff that can be used for stories and whatever."

The spirit sightings have been going on in Lewis's family at least since she was a little girl. After her parents bought a house in which the former owner died, there were a number of strange occurrences.

"There was an old lady that died there in her bed. Her name was Mrs. Chitwood. She loved little kids, and she didn't have any grandchildren. My mom was napping one time on the couch, and she watched a woman walk out of my bedroom and into my brother's room. He was a baby, so I must have been three.

"She said she flew off of that couch and ran in the bedroom. That lady was standing in front of the crib looking at my brother, and she looked at my mom, and she didn't say it out loud, but my mom heard her say, 'I'm just checking on the baby.' That's all I know.

"When I was about three years old, I fell down the stairs from my parents' kitchen to the basement. The basement floor is solid concrete with tile over it. There are thirteen steps. When I fell, I hit nothing on way down, landed at the bottom, looked up laughing and smiled. My mom said there was no way anybody could have made that fall (and not been hurt) without somebody catching them. A thirteen-step drop onto concrete—I didn't even have a bruise.

"The only time I ever saw her was, I walked in the bathroom and she was standing there. My brother was right there with me, and I screamed and ran out. I couldn't describe her face, but she was wearing a white nightgown with puffy sleeves. She didn't look the way my grandpa looked. She looked . . . wispy. I'll never forget that."

As for her own time of dying, Lewis says the idea doesn't particularly bother her. She thinks about it sometimes. The only thing she asks is that it not happen too soon.

"Have you ever heard that song, 'Everybody wants to go to heaven, but nobody wants to go now'? That about sums it up for me.

"I'm not scared to die, [but] do I want to go now? No. I want to be a mom and a grandma. There are places in this world that I want to see—I have a bucket list. But if I found out tomorrow that I was dying, would I be upset? Yes. Would I cuss God and hate the world and everything? No.

"I'm not ready to go yet, but when I've lived my life and had a little bit more time, I'll be ready. Heaven's there waiting. I've seen my version of it already, through my grandpa."

Chapter 18:

Linda Meadors

> *"Buddhists don't have a fear of dying like other people. I know I'm going to come back, so I'm OK with it."*

Lightning did not strike when Thailand native Linda Meadors last entered a church building many years ago, but what did happen convinced her that her spiritual needs would be better met someplace else.

"It was when my father and mother were still married—I had to be about seven or eight—and one of our neighbors came over and asked my mom if I could go to church with them. We were Buddhists, and they were Jehovah's Witness, but my mom said OK, because in Buddhism, they don't chastise you for going to other religions. The whole point of life is to learn. So I go.

"When you walk into the church, there's a little area inside the front doors, and then you go through another set of doors to actually go into the sanctuary part, and there was a huge cross standing up there, and it's backlit and everything, and when I walked in and walked past it, the cross actually fell off the wall and just barely missed me.

"I'm not kidding," Mrs. Meadors said. "That actually happened. Everybody was shocked, because it was bolted to the structure, and it came out and just crashed to the floor. And that was enough. That's the last time I've ever been to any type of church.

"It was scary, but it was also an aha moment, even at that young age. I figured something in the universe was telling me that what I was living was the right way of living, and I knew that I would never need to go [to a church] again."

Mrs. Meadors was born in Bangkok, Thailand and spent the first five years of her life there, the daughter of a Thai mother and a US Army soldier father. Her dad was originally from British Guiana in South America. Now forty-three, married with three kids, she and her family came to the United States for a while, then moved to Germany when her father was stationed there. That was where she first met her husband and fellow army brat, James, who went on to serve twelve years in the military.

It was meeting her husband, in fact, that helped solidify her belief in the Buddhist principles of reincarnation and past life experiences.

"I used to dream that there was this man that I was going to be with, and in these dreams, I could only see his forearms. So I always knew I'd marry a white man, because his forearms were white. And it's the strangest thing—that's what always attracted me to a man, if they were wearing a nice watch. It's so crazy.

"I met my husband in high school, and he had kissed me at my front door when he dropped me off. When I went to bed that night, and I had that dream, it was the whole person—and it was him. I could see him. Any time before, it was just like a fog in the way, and you wanted to just brush the fog away. And this time, I saw him. It was him.

"One night, I had to go walk my dog. In Germany, they use coal to heat everything, so they have these coal elevators, and when you step on it, it sort of moves. James had come to visit, and he went with me. We were holding hands, and we stepped on one of these coal elevators, and at the moment, all of a sudden, I was taken back [in time], and I could see us on a paddlewheel boat. I knew it was me, and I knew it was him, but I wasn't black—you know, black and Thai.

"I was white, and so was he, and I had a locket. I opened the locket and there was a picture of him and I, and I knew it was him and I, but it didn't look anything like us. And I asked him, on the paddlewheel boat, 'Do you know who I am?' And he said, 'Yes.' I said, 'Well, do you know who these other people are?' And he was like, 'Yes.' So I know that we've come back more than once. I believe wholeheartedly that we come back."

Buddhism is one of the world's oldest religions, dating back as far as the sixth century BC. It was founded by Siddhartha Gautama, a warrior prince in Nepal. There are an estimated 1.2 million practitioners in the United States, ranking it well behind Christianity and Judaism in popularity, but approximately equal in numbers with Islam and Hinduism.

American Buddhists include many Asian Americans, along with a large number of converts from other ethnicities. Mrs. Meadors is a practitioner of Theravada Buddhism (Doctrine of the Elders), one of three traditions that also includes Mahayana (Great Vehicle) and Vajrayana (Diamond Vehicle, otherwise known as Tibetan Buddhism).

"I'm thrilled to be Buddhist. It gives me a different perspective on life, I think. I have friends who are Catholic, and they have that Catholic guilt thing going.

"I'm all for those that believe in the Jesus and God situation. You know, yay Jesus, if that makes you a good person, but I just don't ascribe to it. It doesn't make me uncomfortable, but it sometimes makes me sad, because I think they should want to be good people for the same reasons Buddhists want to be good people—because of karma and the good things that come into your life. Whereas Christians want to be good because a book tells them to. There's very few that can really live the life where they want to be good regardless of the book or not."

Practicing Buddhism is not a source of conflict at home, Mrs. Meadors said, even though her husband is a die-hard Baptist. He respects the Buddhist ways but believes personally in his own religion.

"My husband is white as the driven snow, and he is definitely Southern Baptist, but I've known him since high school, so it works out fine. He loves Buddhism. He loves that we don't try to make him a Buddhist. He can come to the temple and they're not going to make him feel bad.

"That's what is really great about Buddhism—it's not a religion that persecutes people. You can be a Buddhist Jewish person or a Buddhist Christian, and the Buddhists aren't going to say anything. They're all for whatever it takes for you to stay on the path, and being good is good enough."

One big thing Buddhism gives her is a lack of fear about dying. She's not afraid at all, because she is absolutely convinced there are more lives to come after this one.

"Buddhists don't have a fear of dying like other people. My husband is terrified. He doesn't want to grow old; he doesn't want to die. He has a huge problem with it. But I don't, because I totally believe 1,000 percent that you come back.

"We tease about it, because Americans believe that you can come back as a bug or something, but you don't come back as an ant or whatever. You come back as another human being. Animals come back as animals, and people come back as people. You come back to learn the lessons that you didn't learn the first time.

"I think if you lived a decent life and you have found peace within your life, you will go peacefully. You know when people have talked about seeing the light, or my grandmother comes to get me . . . I think that is when you're making the transition from one life to the next. I don't think it's heaven. I just think we're placed back in another body, and it's timed perfectly between someone who has died and a child who is born.

"Maybe you grew up as a Christian . . . if that light makes you comfortable to get to the next body, then you see the light. If your grandmother is what's going to make you comfortable with going into your next body, then your grandmother comes to take you to your next life. And I think that's why people see those things. Of course, there are people who say they've seen hell, too. I believe that's because of the way they lived before, and it's something coming to take you to live a crappy life again, until you get it right.

"Buddhists don't have a fear of dying like other people, and for me, I think it's because I know that we come back. I think if you are at peace in your life, then you will die peacefully. Of course, I am afraid to go right now, but the fear is not for me, it's for the ones I'm going to leave behind—my children, for example, and my parents. Parents don't want their children to die before them. But otherwise, no, I have no fear of dying. I just want to make sure that I live a good life."

Chapter 19:

Andy Hermosillo

> *"I feel like my soul might go somewhere, but I don't think it's going to be a situation where I can recognize my family. I think that is just false hope for people to be comforted in losing a loved one."*

For a long time, California native Andy Hermosillo lived by the old adage "eat, drink, and be merry," because he thought his destiny was to die at age thirty-six like his dad.

"My biological father passed away when he was thirty-six years old," Hermosillo said. "He died of a heart attack. He was not healthy; he was an avid drug user. My parents divorced right after I was born. My mom did not want me to be around that.

"So I always thought I would die at thirty-six, because that's when my father died. I would always say that, and my family members would be like, 'No, he lived a different life.' And I just felt like, he was my father, and I'm sure I'm going to die around the same age. Then, once I passed it, I don't even think about death anymore.

"I used to think about it a lot, but now I try not to, because . . . there might be sleepless nights when I do think about it, and it's kind of scary, because I feel this empty, black hole feeling again. It's depressing to me that I'll never see my loved ones again, my friends, the people that I care about. It hurts and it's scary.

"I feel like my soul might go somewhere, but I don't think it's going to be a situation where I can recognize my family. I think that is just false hope for people to be comforted in losing a loved one. I just do not see that happening."

Hermosillo, thirty-nine, was born and raised in San Jose, where he graduated from high school, kicked around for a while taking some community college courses, then went to work for a car dealership. He stayed in the automobile industry for a few years, then started working in hospitality, managing hotels for seven or eight years, and now works in retail.

He grew up going to church with his single-parent mother, but they stopped attending services when his mom met her future second husband.

"My mother and I used to go to church a lot when I was a child—the Christian faith. We went for a while, and then my mom started dating my stepdad, and we stopped going. He wasn't religious and whatnot. I want to say I was about twelve years old when I asked my mom, 'What religion are we?' And she told me I was whatever religion I wanted to be.

"That was so empowering, for her to tell me that—that was just mind blowing for me. All those years going to church, and now I'm whatever religion I want to be?

"I don't know why. I think it's because I missed going to church because I had friends [there], and then when my mom said that, it was like, 'Wow, now I need to find out why. Were we going to the wrong church all along?' I was so confused."

That confusion started a lifelong search for answers that continues today. Hermosillo says he is not a big fan of church and organized religion, but he is constantly searching for answers to life's mysteries.

"When I hear about someone who is very religious, I ask them a lot of questions to see how their religion or faith affects their decision making. I agree with some of it and disagree with some of it.

"I believe in a higher power, and I believe everything is kind of tied into this higher power. I feel like everything circles back to a possible creator. But I don't believe in how certain religions portray their God as a better God, because I believe everything should be one. And it's just a matter of how people interpret it.

"I think if we do good unto others, and we live a good life, and we help our brothers and sisters, I don't see how I can get punished for being a good person, just because I didn't go to church every Sunday, and I didn't make a donation of ten dollars each week. I don't see how that works.

"I've been to church probably a year ago. I have a friend whose father is a pastor at a local church, and every now and then, I'll try to pop in there. I feel like it's really good, as far as spiritual, but I don't agree with a lot of the things they believe in. So, it's interesting, but more to kind of support the family and see what's going on."

Hermosillo, who recently moved to central Texas, lost his mother in August 2014, and never got a chance to say goodbye. He holds out hope for a reunion someday but believes in his heart of hearts that will never happen.

"I ask myself every day, 'Will I ever see her again?' I feel this big, black hole that I'll never see her again.

"My mom was my best friend. And it breaks my heart that she was in California and I wasn't there to spend any last moments with her when she was coherent. By the time I got there and saw her, she was pretty much comatose [and] didn't know I was there.

"So I just want to live life, and live for today. I don't want to take it for granted. When I was younger, I did take it for granted, because I didn't think I would be here. My attitude was, 'Why should I care about my future? I'll probably die, anyway.' My uncles—my dad's brothers—all died of heart attacks in their late thirties. And that's why I was really convinced. I just didn't care, so I lived a very careless lifestyle. Some of the decisions I made, I'm surprised I'm still here.

"Just heavy, heavy drinking . . . binge drinking to where I felt like my liver was going to explode. Thinking I was invincible, you know. Just being stupid . . . how much can I drink? My friend and I would do that, and I'm surprised neither one of us died.

"Now I'm thirty-nine, but I feel like I'm twenty-three, twenty-four years old. I want to travel the world and see more. I had the opportunity a couple of years ago to backpack in Europe for about seven weeks. I never made that a priority before, but I want to get out there and do and see things for my mom that she never got to witness through her own eyes. I've committed to travel more this year. I've booked a trip to go to Italy in March."

For the most part, Hermosillo does not believe in life after death or heaven and hell. He does not consider himself an atheist but sees a lot of problems with things like organized religion and the Bible. Nevertheless, he works hard at keeping an open mind, and still enjoys talking to believers and nonbelievers alike about life's big questions.

"I want to know why. I want to know why I was chosen to be here. Why didn't that other sperm win the race? I wish I knew. Maybe I'll get that answer when I do pass. That would be awesome. In the meantime, who knows?

"I just think people are afraid to realize there is uncertainty [about what happens] after death. So we've created this Disneyland of a heaven to comfort us. You know, hopefully one day I will see my mom again; I will see my dad, who I never met; and I will see passed loved ones. That's comforting, and we want to believe that. But I really don't believe that. I don't see how that physically happens. How can I go to a place I don't believe in?

"Each one of us, I think, tries to portray something that we are comfortable with. Because it is scary to not know what happens after we're gone.

"So I don't believe in life after death. To me, I just don't see how it can happen. I think maybe our spirit goes somewhere, but I don't think we are reincarnated into a body. But I don't know. I think that's a journey we all are on . . . to try and figure out what happens next.

"When I hear about a religion I'm not totally familiar with, I ask questions. Trying to get bits and pieces from each person that I talked to, and kind of trying to form my own views.

"I was once a friend with this girl, and her father was a pastor for about twenty-five years. All of a sudden, he became atheist. When I sat down to talk with him, I asked him, 'How did that happen?' He felt that the church was hypocritical, and it took him awhile to finally see it. He was asking 'Why, why, why?' And they were saying, 'Because it's in the Bible.'

"It was very eye opening for me. That's why I like to ask a lot of questions. There's almost a fear to question the Bible. A hot topic for me is gay marriage. I believe that anyone who loves each other should have the right to marry each other. I think if Jesus is all loving, why is this a sin? That's why I feel sometimes like, yeah, the Bible is hypocritical.

"I know it's kind of hard to talk about religion without people getting offended. That's why I pick and choose who I talk to about these things; just start off with some soft questions and see where it goes. There are times when I feel like I can have a great conversation, because the person is not going to shoot me down and say their way is the right way, and that's it. That's when I get frustrated.

"I don't think that's the purpose of religion. I think we should be able to talk about religion without getting worked up, pointing fingers, and saying, 'No, you're wrong.' We don't really know. We're going off a book written a long time ago . . . that definitely needs to be updated. I don't feel I should live my life according to a book that someone put together. I don't know what their views were when they wrote that book.

"Maybe the purpose of life is to weed out all the good ones and send them to heaven, and weed out all the bad ones and send them to hell—I don't know. I think about it every day when I hear of a young kid dying of cancer. I wonder, 'Why am I still here? Is there a reason?' It breaks my heart when I see these tragic stories of young children dying at nine, ten years old, not even experiencing life. And here I am, just getting through life, trying to figure it out . . . I wonder why that has to happen.

"I feel like if I live a good life and help others in need, I feel like there will be an ultimate prize at the end for me."

Chapter 20:

Stacey Kelsey

> *"My only fear is that I won't live my best life while I am here, but I'm not afraid of death itself."*

Montana native Stacey Kelsey has little use for organized religion and does not believe in places called heaven and hell, but she does think there is such a thing as eternal life.

"I believe the soul has everlasting life," the forty-seven-year-old hypnotherapist says. "I believe our spirit goes into the spirit realm, and that experience is whatever you want it to be, whatever the soul needs. It could decide to come back to Earth or stay in the spirit realm.

"I was raised Lutheran. Lots of guilt and judgment about what was right and wrong. It shied me away from organized religion. I went to church until I was about ten years old. I don't go now because I haven't found one that resonates with me.

"I don't believe in heaven or hell—that they are places. Not in the way that it's talked about in religion. I believe heaven and hell are what we make of them. We create experiences based on belief. So if someone believes they will go to hell, they will, but only because that's the experience they choose for themselves. We create our realities and experiences.

"I believe when we leave our body, we connect to oneness and have an experience as energy. I believe in a higher source vibration that is in all of us, and I call it God, but I don't believe that God is outside of us."

Her belief system has evolved from her early religious training into what it is now as a result of all her life experiences, Kelsey explained, including her brother's tragic, self-inflicted death. Thinking about her own death someday is not a scary proposition, but she is concerned about those she leaves behind.

"I am not afraid to die. I think I will become omnipresent when I die, and that's exciting to me. My only fear is that I won't live my best life while I am here, but I'm not afraid of death itself.

"I had a brother commit suicide. It affected me mostly by watching how it affected everyone in the family. Grief is much more powerful than dying. What is left behind is painful.

"I think about what I was brought up to believe—that I had to fear God; that He was outside of me. I had to learn from my own experiences what my true definition of God is—that God is the connection we have to all things.

"Life is an experience, and whatever you want to experience will happen in your life. I feel the soul comes to earth [solely] for experiences.

"I feel every event in my life has led up to my views. The good ones and the bad ones. I have always had an inner knowing that there is more than what we see and that the universe or God shows us signs . . . so as long as we remain with our senses and heart open, all events allow for the expansion of our soul."

Chapter 21:

Ingeborg Baltussen

> *"I don't believe in life after death. I think that life is now and that I am living it."*

Amsterdam resident Ingeborg Baltussen does not believe in God, but says that religious texts like the Christian Bible contain excellent lessons and principles for living, and she tries her best to follow many of those ideas.

"I am not anti-religion—I find it quite fascinating, actually," Baltussen says. "Makes me even jealous sometimes. Must be wonderful to accept things as the will of some higher being, and being able not to question that decision."

A native of Zaandam, The Netherlands, the forty-five-year-old foundation director and mediator was raised with one sister by a Catholic father and a Protestant mother. Theirs was not a religious home, but her parents sent her to Sunday school at the only church in their small village, about ten kilometers north of Amsterdam.

She was not baptized, as her parents wanted to leave that decision to her. By the time she reached high school age, she went to church with some friends for several years but never felt comfortable and eventually stopped going altogether.

"I just did not and could not believe in God. The Bible was full of beauty, but also nonsense. I argued a lot with the minister, who had explanations or interpretations of the Bible with which

I did not agree at all. I started to feel more and more like a cheat, so one day I decided that enough was enough and stopped going. I was seventeen years old. I have never regretted that moment, nor have I doubted it.

"At the age of thirty-one, I came to work for a National Christian Labour Union. Almost all my colleagues were Christian. I worked there for seven years, and I had to take courses in Christian social history and management. I also did a masterclass of two years. I was the only one in our group that did not believe in God.

"In the end, a very religious classmate told me that he had had his reservations against me, since I did not get my values out of the Bible. After two years, he had found that I actually knew the Bible quite well and had never been disrespectful of his faith or his beliefs. We had had quite a few discussions, and we are still in contact. The rest of my colleagues often said to me that I was more of a Christian than they were because I was actually quite strict in following the specific Christian lines within our union.

"For instance, sustainability was a big thing, because we are responsible to leave an Earth that is still livable to the generations to come: stewardship. Or the way I negotiated, with respect to my opponent, but tough on the interest at hand.

"I find it difficult sometimes to understand why somebody calls himself a Christian and goes to church every Sunday, but then behaves in a way that I think is not in line with that religion. And I don't mean murder and theft, but without love or care."

She cannot accept the existence of God or a higher power for a number of reasons, Baltussen says, including what she sees as massive "inequality" throughout the world, along with a large number of fanciful tales filling the Bible. Heaven and hell, meanwhile, are places created by people right here on Earth, she says, through the way they lives their lives, and the choices and decisions they make.

"There are two sides to the question of why I don't believe in God. The first one is on a logical level.

"I find the Bible a very interesting book with many beautiful stories, but it is impossible to be true. The way it came to be written, for one . . . everyone that ever did the game of telling a story to some people and asking them to retell the story to another person entering the room, and have that last entering person tell it to another new person entering the room, knows that after four people, there is nothing left of the original story. After another four people, so many new items were added that it has become a whole new story, by itself. And, also, the translation difficulties, the political meddling at times, and so on.

"The stories themselves are also filled with impossibilities, and especially the Old Testament is filled with fairy tales. The New Testament has wonderful life lessons in it, and my favorite is King Solomon.

"But apart from the Bible, I don't believe that a God would be responsible for an Earth with so much inequality. It would make it a racist God; a cruel God; a powerless God, for him not being able to stop, for instance, a Holocaust or Boko Haram, horrible famine in Africa, the Hutus against the Tutsis, and so on.

"How can you believe in a God that would give me, for being born in The Netherlands, a happy and healthy life, and the African child born on the same day in Ethiopia, a life full of war and famine? Especially since that Ethiopian child and its parents probably believe in God, even though they have no reason whatsoever to do so. And why would homosexual people be wrong if there is a God that created man to its image and is considered flawless.

"I once asked a religious person who told me homosexuality is a sin if it could not be God's way to prevent the earth from overpopulating? So no, I don't believe in a God. But, having said that, I do think that most people agree with the commandments that you should not kill or steal. And be kind to others, and be faithful and not to lie. And even though it is not always easy to stick to them, I still think most people in their hearts think this is how they should behave.

"God, for me, is a mythical figure that has been made up by people ages ago to understand certain things happening. I see people using their God as an excuse to justify all kinds of [bad] behavior and deeds."

The cigar-loving Dutch woman says she thinks what is most important is listening to her heart, which always lets her know what is right and what is wrong. That quiet voice is inside everyone, she says, and can guide our decisions as well as or better than anything else.

With no God, no heaven or hell, no anything coming after this life, Baltussen believes the purpose of this existence is basically to be the best person you can be. To have goals and work to achieve them. To treat others as you wish to be treated. To love and be loved.

"I don't think that there is a higher purpose. I do think that we can achieve wonderful things. I also think that you can give your life purpose yourself. Again, think about the kind of person you are or want to be, and what you would like to achieve.

"I try to listen to my heart, because I know by now that it is always right. If something feels good, I know it is. More important, if something doesn't feel good, it really isn't. I think we have become very good at listening to our head instead of our heart. Reasoning, explaining to ourselves why something is not wrong. We are able to very honestly corrupt ourselves. Explain to ourselves that it is right to sell financial products to people even though we know that we might bring them in great financial problems. Talk ourselves into big bonuses, or into cheating on our spouse. In our heart, we know it is wrong, but we have become really good at ignoring that inner voice.

"If I have to call something God, I think it is that inner voice. For me, it is very important to live according to that voice, that feeling, that notion. Doing things for people because I want to, not because I have something to gain. Being able to always look straight at myself in the mirror. Treating people like I want to be treated myself. Do good unto others when possible. And, especially since I think our lives are now, we have to be like that now. Not because of a reward after death, but because you can.

"I think that life is now and that I am living it. After I die, I will just either rot away in the ground or, my preference, burn in a furnace at a funeral home. I don't believe in life after death or a higher being or a God. I do believe, however, that here on Earth there is more 'energy' than we notice. And I don't mean of ghosts or spirits, but of what we ourselves radiate. We have become very mind- and thought-centered, and sometimes forget about feeling and heart. I think we can be more susceptible to senses that we radiate and feel more of what is happening with people. I think it has to do with love. Opening your heart to feel starts with love."

As for the prospect of her own death, Baltussen says she is not afraid, but hopes to be in control of her own destiny. She supports euthanasia, which is legal in her country. She is a member of a euthanasia organization.

"I am not afraid to die. I am afraid, however, to die slowly and painfully. I don't think that such suffering is necessary.

"I recently started thinking about it, but especially about my funeral, or rather cremation, and my will. I am not in contact anymore with my parents and sister, so I want to make a will to make sure that my two best friends can make decisions for me. I do believe that people should have the right to decide for themselves how and when they would like to die.

"Even though euthanasia is possible, it is not simple. There has to be intolerable suffering, and a doctor should administer the drugs to end the life. This puts a large strain on doctors. I find it fascinating how we think that death is something you cannot choose; that we think somebody is out of his mind if he says he wants to die.

"Whenever somebody my age or younger dies, it reminds me of how lucky I am to be healthy and happy. I don't mind that I am forty-five years old. I don't have to lie about my age."

Chapter 22:

Jim M.

> *"I believe our soul leaves our body and goes to either heaven or hell. If we have loved as God intended us to do, our soul goes to heaven. If we have lived in hate, then we would be doomed to hell."*

North Carolina resident Jim M. has suffered enough trials, tribulations, and tragedies to last several lifetimes.

At age three, he was given last rites by a Catholic priest. He grew up with an alcoholic mother and was sexually abused at a young age. While serving in the US Army, he survived a mortar attack and being shot down twice in Vietnam. Later, he lost a teenage son to cancer and endured two divorces, ongoing estrangement from his daughters, and his own bout with prostate cancer. Although his faith and beliefs were understandably rocked at times by these challenges, the sixty-seven-year-old says he has always turned back to God in the end for strength and guidance.

"Each of these things made me stronger and brought me closer to God," says Jim, who asked that his last name not be used. "The purpose of life is to do God's will on Earth, spreading his love any way we can. Life is love, for love does."

While he has certainly seen more than his own share of difficulties, Jim says he believes God has always been with him, including the night he nearly died when he was a toddler.

"I had to have an emergency tracheotomy in the middle of the night. At that time, I received the sacrament of Extreme Unction, also known as the last sacrament or last rites. Today, this sacrament is known as Unction, or the sacrament of healing, or anointing of the sick, and is not reserved simply for life and death situations. When I look back, I believe God had a special plan for me then, which kept me strong in my faith."

Jim was raised in a Catholic home with an older brother and two older sisters. His mother was what he describes as an "extreme" alcoholic.

"From my earliest memories, I knew about my mother," he explains. "She was not abusive to me, but a peaceful and sad drunk. My father had her committed three times to get sober and receive help. Each time she entered treatment, she promised she'd stay sober, but once she got back home . . . within three weeks or so, she would be right back to her addict behaviors: hiding vodka in perfume bottles, shoe boxes, shoes, and anywhere else she thought we could not find the alcohol.

"When I was in the third and fourth grade, she would take me out of school for a week at a time to go to the mountains, where she would drink most of the day. The local priest would come over for cocktails and get drunk with her, as well, leaving me to fend for myself. This caused me to question our clergy.

"As soon as I could, I became an altar boy and started going to Mass daily. I didn't really understand all of this at the time, but I did know that when I went to Mass and received the Eucharist, as well as going to confession weekly, I'd felt better, and I knew that God was there to help me and not condemn me. I even did nine first Fridays, which in the fifties and early sixties was going to Mass and receiving the Eucharist nine months in a row on the first Friday of the month. In the Catholic Church, if you made nine first Fridays, you would automatically go to heaven. Now, I've got my free pass.

"During this time, as my own faith deepened, and as I felt more secure in my own spiritual life, I began to reach out to friends that were struggling with issues of faith or who were making poor choices. I encouraged my friends to go to church to receive the sacraments and to go to confession.

"My high school years brought additional challenges. Mom was drunk every night. Dinners were regular arguments between my parents. Many nights the argument was about which side of the family had the most drunks. My brother and sisters had moved out by now, and most of the time, either my dad or I had to fix dinner. When my mother tried to make dinner, it was usually burned.

"The worst day was in March of my senior year in high school. My father was at a medical convention in Chicago and my mother was to meet him in Las Vegas with some family friends. The day before she was to leave, I came home and found her drunk. She was on the couch with a drink that she said was water. I tasted the drink and discovering it was straight vodka; I threw it in her face. I told her how much I hated her and wished her dead. She tried to stand up but couldn't, so I carried her upstairs and threw her on her bed.

"The next morning at the breakfast table, she asked that I bring down her luggage. I did but not without telling her off about the night before, and again telling her how much I hated her and wished she was dead. Her last words to me were that she knew I did not mean it and that someday I would regret what I was saying.

"Later that day, at lunch, our school principal, Brother John, stopped me and asked that I help him with some books in his office. Once there, he told me my mother had died and was found by our neighbor at the breakfast room table, where I had left her. I hit the wall with my fist but could not cry. I was thinking, 'Thank God.'"

With his father remarrying twice over the next two years, Jim went off to college in Spokane, Washington, but struggling with his relationship with God, he decided to join the army after the first semester of his sophomore year at the Catholic university.

The next nine years were a "rollercoaster."

After being stationed in Germany, he volunteered to go fight in the Vietnam War. It was there that he met a chaplain who helped him iron out some of his spiritual questions. He received a Purple Heart and Bronze Star, completed his first three-year hitch in the army, and was accepted to flight school. His next duty assignment was at Fort Bragg, North Carolina, where he met his first wife, who had two young children, which he later adopted.

Jim then volunteered for another tour in Vietnam, and later resigned from the military after nine years' service when he and his wife had a baby.

"I had done what I could do," he says. "I earned thirty-five air medals, the Distinguished Flying Cross, and had risked my life and faced death more than a few times. I wanted to pursue a career in business and was looking to make big bucks! Of course, all of these decisions were being made without asking for God's help."

He went to work for a company in the Midwest, bought a home, enrolled the kids in Catholic school, and started going back to church. After completing a degree in business management, he was promoted and accepted a job in Texas in 1982.

One day at work, his son's football coach from school called Jim and told him the boy's leg was "really hurting" and he probably should see a doctor. X-rays showed a tumor, and a subsequent biopsy at Baylor Cancer Center resulted in a diagnosis of osteosarcoma, bone cancer.

That was in August, and the next two months were a whirlwind "heaven and hell" of trips back and forth to MD Anderson hospital in Houston. After seven weeks of chemotherapy and radiation treatments, doctors wanted to amputate to stop the spread of the disease. They let him go home for a week before the surgery, and the young boy told his dad he did not want his leg removed.

"A really tough moment for me was one day when my son and I had time together, just the two of us. He expressed to me that he didn't want his leg amputated and was ready to die if it was God's will. He asked me not to tell his mother. During his time at the hospital, I learned how courageous the children were. They knew what they were facing, and they talked freely with each other about cancer and death.

"My son and his mother left on Sunday morning to return to Houston, and the amputation was scheduled for the next Wednesday. Sunday night, I got a call that he was in a coma and that his kidneys were failing. I called a neighbor who took me to the airport for the next flight to Houston. At the hospital, his primary doctor called us in and explained that he could put him on a dialysis machine, which would keep him alive, but he could not say for how long. The kidney failure was being caused by the cancer. In a CAT scan done that morning, cancer had also been discovered in other parts of my son's body. Our choice was to either keep him alive in limbo on dialysis or let him die from the kidney failure. We chose to let our son go to be with God.

"The next few hours were spent by his bedside, praying and asking God to keep him from feeling pain. When the time came, I was holding his hand and told him God was waiting and it was OK to let go. It was eight weeks from the cancer being detected.

"I could not believe the anger I felt. 'Why not me, God? Why do you take a boy of thirteen, full of life, with the world before him, rather than me?'

"I had done two tours in Vietnam, and there had been times I had been close to death. God let me live. I was older and I'd had a full life and experienced many things. After calling home and notifying the family of his death, I ripped the phone out of the wall and threw it across the room."

Jim reached out to God and to his church to deal with the boy's death, while his wife withdrew from everyone and everything. After two years of counseling, talking, and prayer, the couple decided to divorce. He did not see much of his two daughters after that, and their relationship remains strained.

Five years later, he married again, mostly because he was desperately lonely, and in March 1998, Jim found out he had prostate cancer. This and ongoing financial problems led to his second divorce, and also to volunteer work with the American

Cancer Society and some very important friendships, along with a renewed commitment to his religious faith.

"I attended a workshop held by an Episcopal priest on the ministry of Healing at All Saints. This led to a great change in my life. I went and spent three days for a spiritual healing of my soul to deal with the hurt, remorse, and anger feelings I had suppressed over the years from my mother's death and my father's marriages. With guidance and the power of the Holy Spirit, I was able to forgive myself through the visions I experienced with Christ standing by my side, with my mother and father separately.

"My life is like many others. I've never considered myself a pious individual, but I do know that every time God put challenges in my life—whether it be my mother's death, Vietnam, my best friend's death, the loss of my son, two divorces, cancer—I would reach out to God for strength through prayer, the sacraments, and religious counseling, and my faith would grow even stronger.

"No matter how much grief and sadness that you may have in your life, God will create so much more good that will outweigh all the difficult times," says Jim, who has four grandchildren and three great-grandchildren.

"I'm just a man wanting to do whatever God guides me to do. Religious, one might say, yes, but being a cradle Catholic, a baptized Baptist, and a confirmed Episcopalian, I have realized man created religions, and what is first and foremost is living by Christ's two great commandments: 'Thou shalt love the Lord thy God with thy whole heart, and with thy whole soul, and with thy whole mind, and with thy whole strength; and Thou shalt love thy neighbor as thyself.'

"Life after death to me is our greatest reward in that we go into the arms of Christ after we have completed his mission for him on earth. I truly look forward to it."

Chapter 23:

Vanessa Rivera

> *"My hope is that life after death would be . . . like when you're in a really deep sleep, and you're in a really good dream."*

Born and raised in Queens, New York, the daughter of a secretary mother and an alcoholic, sometimes employed, sometimes violent father, Vanessa Rivera grew up going to church, attending parochial school, and even enrolled in a Lutheran college, but a lifetime of hurts and disappointments has left her questioning all those early beliefs.

"I still consider myself spiritual," the fifty-six-year-old mother of one says. "I was much more so years ago, but I think sometimes life just beats it out of you.

"I bought it lock, stock, and barrel back then, but over time . . . I don't know. I think everyone has some crisis of faith, depending on circumstances or situations that might happen to them, and there were a few for me that really rocked my world to the point where I can absolutely understand when people say it's much easier to not believe in God. That way, life is just random, and there's no expectation that there should be some type of order.

"So, I'm not really sure where I fall these days on the spectrum of how much I believe. I think it's so ingrained in me that I want to believe. I want to believe that there's a higher power who wants to make sure that we have good lives, but I don't know.

"I sure as hell hope there's life after death. There better be something better than this," she says, laughing.

Rivera describes her upbringing as blue collar, working class. Her dad was a handyman who wasn't much interested in keeping a job, so her mom was the primary breadwinner. She and her late sister, Yvette, were active in church and mostly stayed out of trouble. When she was sixteen, Vanessa graduated from high school and headed out to Nebraska to attend a college recommended by her biology teacher and his wife. She was close to the couple and trusted their guidance, so off she went, from the streets of the Big Apple to the cornfields of the Midwest.

"What the hell does a sixteen-year-old know? Nothing," she said. "You talk about culture shock. It was a trip. I was really, really lonely. I did not last even a semester."

After about seven weeks of attending classes, Rivera was on her way back to New York. Two years later, she married one of her former high school teachers. She was 18; he was 31. She went to work as a secretary and had a baby. The marriage lasted three years.

"Bad, bad, bad," she says. "Poor choices. He was a raging alcoholic. When I think back on it now, it wasn't a marriage. It wasn't a relationship. I don't know what it was. It was bizarre."

After working various clerical jobs and moving for a while to Pennsylvania, Rivera eventually went back to school and earned a bachelor's degree and a master's degree. The Columbia University graduate now works as an assistant principal for the New York City public school system.

While her life from the outside looking in would appear to be quite successful, Rivera admits to being lonely, even living in a city of nine million people. And some of the emotional body blows she has endured over the years would be enough to bring many people to their knees.

Her mother died of uterine cancer when Vanessa was ten years old. Her sister, Yvette, died forty years later of the same thing, three years after their father's death.

She never got to say goodbye to her father or her sister.

"It was when we were in our twenties," Vanessa explains, "when my sister met someone on the train, here in the city. He was a medical student from Egypt, and one day, they up and moved to Egypt, got married, and never came back. I never saw her again.

"I called her office one day, and they said, 'Oh, hi, she's not here. She's in Egypt.' I didn't think too much about it, because she worked for a travel agency—this was in the mid-1980s; early eighties—and she was always flitting all over the place. So it was not unusual for her to be gone.

"A week goes by and I call back, and one of the gals in her office says to me, 'Oh, Vanessa, she's in Egypt.' I said, 'Yeah, but when is she coming back?' And there was dead silence on the phone. The girl said, 'They got married, and she moved.'

"You could have knocked me over with a feather. Are you kidding me? As much as my sister and I used to fight, I was just blown away."

She tried to contact her sister at various times over the years without success, and then in February 2009, she found out via e-mail that her sister had died the year before.

"It was from one of her daughters—she had two daughters, and in going through their mom's things, they found an envelope with all of this stuff, including her high school yearbook and cards that I sent her that she opened but never responded to. There were photographs of the two of us together.

"They didn't know that their mom had a sister. She never told them. But they put two and two together, and they found me on Facebook. There's like nine hundred Vanessa Riveras in New York City, and they wrote to every single one."

Then there was her father. She had not seen him in about five years when she got a phone call saying he was sick and in the hospital. By the time she got there, it was too late.

"My dad was a strange bird. He had remarried—he had a couple of different wives—and he did not really want to have a normal life. He drank a lot, and he lived sort of like a bum for a long time. In these weird rooms. In vacant apartments. And no matter what I tried to do to help the situation, he just refused any kind of help.

"For many years, when I was living in Pennsylvania, I would invite him to come out for the weekend—he didn't drive, so I said I would come and get him—and he never wanted to. He did not want to have a relationship like that with his children, I don't think. Or he wasn't able to, I don't know.

"Sometimes I think we were like a part of his past. And, honestly, he wasn't a nice person when I was a kid. My parents had a very volatile relationship—the police were at our house all the time. He was pretty violent, and so there was a lot of not-good feelings there.

"When he died—this was in 2005—I was here in New York, and his wife called me and she said, 'He's in the hospital; he's very sick.' I lived about an hour and a half away from the hospital, so I got in the car and off I went. By the time I got there, he had passed. She's there, and her two sons are there, so I'm talking to her and I go to ask about the funeral and she won't tell me where the funeral is going to be, because I've been such a horrible daughter.

"She would call me periodically and yell at me for not calling my father and not being a good daughter, and blah, blah, blah. I would be like, 'OK, lady, you have no freakin' clue. You have no idea what this man has done.'

"I would say to her, 'You're kidding me, right?' I used to send him money. When my daughter was little, we used to go visit him at Christmas. Sometimes we'd get there, and he wouldn't be home. He'd be in the bar somewhere, or he'd be somewhere else. So I always thought it was kind of funny that his wife would chastise me for being a terrible daughter.

"So she wouldn't tell me where the funeral was. I said, 'Okey dokey.' I explained to her that I was sorry she felt that way. She only saw one side of my dad. She didn't know him from age forty to age sixty. She only knew him from age sixty to age seventy. And that was the end of that. I never saw her again after that. And I certainly never saw my dad again.

"It must have affected me on some level—I don't know in what way. I guess one would say that there was no closure, and that was my last chance."

As far as her own death someday, Rivera says she thinks about that quite often. She is not obsessed with the idea, but she thinks about it.

"Oh, yeah," she said. "I try to figure out who's going to be sad. Who would be sad if I died? Will anybody give two hoots? I also think about how random death is.

"And I have this theory, not so much about dying, but about how people view death. I've known a lot of people who are afraid of death. They don't want to die, they don't want any of their friends to die, and when people that they know die, they are wailing and moaning and crying, and it's such a big deal. And I look at them and I say, 'Why are you getting so upset? They were, like, ninety-four years old.'

"My theory is, I believe that if you experience death in your life out of sequence—for instance, my mom died when I was little, and parents aren't supposed to die when their kids are little, so it's out of sequence; a parent loses a child, and kids aren't supposed to die before their parents, so that's out of sequence; a young newlywed, their spouse is killed at age thirty or something, that's out of sequence—if you experience the death of a loved one out of sequence, you are much more understanding of the randomness of it. The fact that it can happen at any second. And you can't get pissed off about it.

"I'm not saying people shouldn't get upset when somebody dies—of course you're going to get upset—but they have this kind of . . . what I perceive from my experience as this overly emotional reaction to it. And I'll ask them, 'How many people have died in your life?' They say, 'No one.' Or if people have died, it's always been in sequence. You know, 'My grandfather died.' 'How old was he?' 'Eighty-seven.' 'My aunt died.' 'How old was she?' 'Ninety-three.' So they haven't been able to figure out a way to deal with it better."

When she was a kid, Rivera believed in heaven and hell, God sitting on his throne, angels singing songs in eternal paradise. Some people go to heaven; some people go to hell. Now, she's not so sure about any of it.

"That's the vision that so many of us grew up with. My only problem with that vision is that it's too much like here. You know, you're up there and you live on a cloud—God has the biggest cloud—and then how is everyone else organized? Who gets to sit on which cloud, and why is that cloud closer to the cloud where God is?

"That's why I'd rather think of life after death like being in a dream. Not in the same physical space or body that we're in now, obviously, but sort of like when you're dreaming. Not waking up, and not wanting to wake up. Like when you're in a really deep sleep, and you're in a really good dream. You're not awake, but you're experiencing things—feelings, emotions, physical sensations.

"I guess my sense is, if it's not some pretty village up in the clouds where everybody is wearing a white robe and a halo, that it's kind of a peaceful sleep where you just feel joy. I hope death is a peaceful place, whether it's the joyful sleep or up in the clouds.

"However, as much as I'm not afraid of death, I'm not ready for that peaceful sleep, either. I still want to feel some more of life. If this is it, I want to just enjoy it as long as it lasts, and continue to try and find a way to be happy."

Chapter 24:

Salma Falah

"I'll die one day, but my soul won't."

Salma Falah grew up in a Muslim family in North Africa and believes that she will earn a place in heaven or hell partly through her actions here on Earth.

"I do believe in life after death, because it is mentioned in the Quran and Sunnah," says Falah, twenty, who is now a sophomore university student studying English in Morocco. "I'm convinced that I'll die one day, but my soul won't.

"When God orders for someone to die, two angels come to catch the person's life. If he's a good person, those two angels look white, shining, and with good smell. The angel meant to catch lives catches it so easily and takes it to the seventh sky, in order to be written as died. A handsome guy comes and shows the soul its place in heaven, and the grave become larger with good smell.

"If the dying person is bad, two ugly angels come and stay in front of him as an alert for the angel who is responsible in taking lives. Once he comes, with a scary face he takes the person's life with effort, and takes it to the seventh sky to be written as dead. On his way, the soul smells nasty, and the angel is insulting it. Once he gets there, God closes the sky, and the angel throws the soul to the grave. The grave starts getting smaller and the soul sees its place in hell.

"Before the person sees whether he goes to hell or heaven, two other angels come to ask: 'Who's your God; your prophet; your religion; and who taught you that?' After answering those questions, the guy comes to show the soul its place, according to what he has done in his life and his answers. The souls then go back into the grave to await resurrection and judgment day."

Ms. Falah, the eldest of three girls in her family, says she believes God is the creator of all life. She used to go to mosque frequently for study and worship, but is now occupied mostly by her studies.

According to missionislam.com, there are six basic Muslim beliefs:

1. There is one true God.
2. Angels are honored creatures who worship and obey God, and act on his command. Among the angels is Gabriel, who brought down the Quran to Muhammad.
3. God revealed books to his messengers as guidance for mankind, including the Qur'an, which was revealed to the prophet Muhammad.
4. Prophets, including Adam, Noah, Abraham, Ishmael, Isaac, Jacob, Moses, and Jesus, revealed God's final message to man to the prophet Muhammad. Muslims believe that all the prophets and messengers were created human beings who had none of the divine qualities of God.
5. All people will be resurrected for God's judgment according to their beliefs and deeds.
6. Muslims believe in Divine Predestination, but also that human beings have free will, given by God. This means they can choose right or wrong, and they are responsible for their choices. The belief in Divine Predestination includes four things: God knows everything, what has happened and what will happen; God has recorded all that has happened and all that will happen; whatever God wills to happen happens, and whatever He wills not to happen does not happen; God is the creator of everything.

"I consider myself a religious person, because I'm Muslim; I believe in God and try to respect what was said and avoid what's forbidden. I also consider myself spiritual, because religion is based on spirituality.

"I believe that all human beings, creatures, plants, even a fly, is created by God," Ms. Falah explained. "I am convinced it's by a higher power. I believe in heaven and hell because that was mentioned in Quran and Sunnah, and as a Muslim it is a part of my religion. And, also, as it's known in life, there is bad and good people, so bad should be punished and good should be rewarded.

"I used to go to the mosque to learn the Quran and Hadith, but I quit now, being busy in studying. I do pray—and quit sometimes due to my laziness—from the mistakes I did, and I ask God to forgive me.

"Just by reading the Quran, I discovered some miracles that even scientists admit, even though those things were said years ago, they just found in the twenty-first century. So, I'm convinced with my religion. I'm satisfied that whenever I face a problem, I go cry and ask God for solving my wonders."

Chapter 25:

Claude Tranchant

> *"I think we need to prepare ourselves for this transition; we all know that there is no escape."*

Claude Tranchant was more than 10,500 miles away when her father died, and in that instant she felt his spirit arrive to comfort her.

"I was born in France and have been living in Australia for the past thirty-five years," Ms. Tranchant explains. "I was at my home in Australia when my father passed away in France. I knew this event had taken place before receiving my sister's phone call, as I felt the arms of my father around me at the time of his death, and we cried in togetherness."

Born and raised in Aix-les-Bains, France, with one brother and one sister, sixty-eight-year-old Tranchant is a self-publisher and author of the book *Boots to Bliss*, the story of her walk four years ago along the Camino de Santiago pilgrimage. She started her solo backpacking journey in Vezelay, in the Burgundy region of France, hiked across the country and over the Pyrenees Mountains, then all the way across northern Spain to Santiago de Compostela, finally finishing one hundred days later at Muxia, for a total distance of roughly twenty-five hundred kilometers. All on her own.

On her website, bootstobliss.com, Tranchant, who was not an experienced trekker, says, "When I returned, I was a free, strong, and determined human being. I had learnt a lot about the human spirit and the power of being, and to live in the moment."

She has believed in life after death from an early age, Tranchant says. A particularly moving and memorable experience occurred when she was four or five years old:

"It is still very vivid in my mind," she said. "During the summer holidays, when I was a small child, I used to go and stay with my parents' relatives in the country. A relative or friend had died. In those days, a car was a luxury, [so] my parents' relative and I walked across the fields, along a path, to the home of the deceased.

"After we arrived, we were led to a bedroom. I saw a man lying on top of the bed. He was dressed in a black suit and had his hands joined together, like he was praying. I was asked to come close to the bed, and to give him a kiss. I obeyed and, shyly, I approached the bed, then someone lifted me up and I kissed his cold face. The sensation of the coldness is still within me to this day.

"Even at this early age, I understood the meaning of death. This had a profound effect on me, which still remains nowadays. I have a very deep connection with the dying and their family. And, amazingly, in the later part of my life, I am volunteering now in palliative care (similar to hospice care) at a hospital. I can feel my heart opening to the fullest towards the dying and they seem to sense my unconditional love, as I can bring them a feeling of calmness. Maybe if I had not had this early experience, I would not have found, later on, my life purpose."

She believes in God, life after death, heaven and hell. God is the creator of the universe, Tranchant says, and he wants people to be happy and joyful. She communicates with God through prayer, and considers herself both religious and spiritual.

"I can't see how you can separate the two. Religion offered me the platform to grow spiritually. It is a way of loving [and] accepting God, as well as my fellow men and the world, with an open heart.

"I believe in God, the biggest power, a loving God, who pours his love on us, no matter what. When I hear the word 'God,' I hear the words 'life' and 'love.' The scientific theory of evolution is demonstrating that things evolve and change, therefore God can't exist. I would say, why not accept this theory of evolution and still believe in God?

"I pray—not in a religious sense, but rather as a spiritual connection. My prayers are private conversations with God—when I see a beautiful butterfly, when I marvel at the beauty of nature, of a flower, of an animal, a landscape; when I am sad, when I am worried, when I am happy. My prayers connect me with God. I believe in the power of prayer.

"I think after our death, there is a time of transition between this life and the next one, which will lead us to God. I think we need to prepare ourselves for this transition; we all know that there is no escape. The two things in this life we are sure of are: birth and death.

"And though I believe God is loving, compassionate, forgiving, nonjudgmental, I presume he must have some laws. I think heaven is where infinite love exists. Hell is where you will relive how your actions, your words, have affected others and where you will feel the pain you have inflicted. I believe God has given us the freedom of choice, and hell is where you reap the consequences of your unloving actions.

"I do think about my own dying. Now, I am not afraid, but who knows at the time of death how I will react.

"When I reflect on my life, I see the changes; I see the mistakes I have made as missed opportunities to learn how to grow in love, creating deeper meanings in my life. I look for fulfillment and for a meaningful purpose in life coming from love. Outside of my 'normal' existence, I look for a life that will nourish my soul, bring me peace, happiness, love, and compassion.

"I know whatever happened in my life was meant to be. It was an opportunity to 'grow' in love."

Chapter 26:

Randy Dyer

> *"If you're going to talk about dying, you also have to talk about living . . . because that's part and parcel, one to the other. You can't die if you haven't lived."*

Dying is not something that Kansas native Randy Dyer is particularly concerned about. He knows it's going to happen, sure, but what he does while he's alive is of much more consequence to him than what happens after he is dead.

"There's a whole bunch of different belief systems, and it's all about dealing with life and dealing with death," Dyer says. "As far as I can tell, we have to get through life to get to death. I have no control over death, so the idea that I can do something here to impact the other side over there, I don't know that I have that capacity. I don't know that I have that power.

"My thing is, life is all about choices. I don't know that I can affect anything after my chemical-electrical stimulus stops happening between my ears, but I know I can impact everything between point A and point B. So that's what I do. The idea of what happens after, it's out of my control.

"When I die, there may be something out there. There may be a nirvana. There may be a purgatory. There may be a heaven and there may be a hell. Nobody has definitive proof of any of that. In the Bible, they called some guy that had some problems making the mental leap for that, they called him Doubting Thomas.

"There's a saying: 'Fight the fight worth winning; fight the fight worth fighting.' You have little control over what happens after you die. You have little control over anything that happens prior to your being born. What you have control over is everything in between. And you've got to get through it. How do you do that? That's what I'm concerned about."

Dyer, a fifty-year-old computer systems engineer, spent twelve years in the National Guard and eight years in the army before retiring from the service in 2000. He was born into a devoutly Baptist, all-American family in Kansas City. Life was simple and good until young Randy was about six years old. Then, a devastating event turned his world upside down.

"My mother got cancer, and I watched her be consumed by the cancer. She died when I was six, maybe seven. Historically, through centuries, the family unit was very close, because people didn't move fifty miles from where they were born. Mothers, fathers, grandparents were all very closely knit—and there was a lot of watching people die. So, it was a whole process of dealing with life while watching people die.

"But as we have moved into these more modern ages, we travel around and so some of that family knit isn't as close as it used to be, back in the day. But . . . my dad had gotten a hospital bed and put it in the front room, and so for a period of time, our world essentially centered around my mother being consumed by cancer, until it got to the point where she had to go to the hospital for the last few days.

"That was pretty traumatic as a young kid, to see that progress. It's very hard for a kid to understand, and my dad was a young married guy with two young kids, and I'm sure he didn't really understand how to deal with it, either.

"There was a huge transition problem, going from the truly nuclear family—mom and dad, brother and sister—and then mom is gone. Now, dad still has to be the guy going to work, bringing home the prototypical bacon, but back at the house, there's no mother figure to take up that role. And my dad had no wherewithal for that. He had no capacity to take on the mother role.

"So, watching that happen was pretty intense. There were some other family members that tried to step in from time to time to try and pick up those mother pieces that had fallen. But that was very inconsistent and almost nonexistent."

But it was not only the pain and sorrow and confusion of losing his mother that had a profound effect. Not long after she died, everything he had been taught to believe about God and religion—and the world—seemed to fly out the window.

"In Kansas, there's really no Southern Baptists, so we were just Baptists. That was the mechanism that my dad grew up with and that was how he dealt with life. And in the Baptist religion—and I guess Protestant, in general—the mentality is that there is the Savior, the Christ, and there's a process that you go through dealing with him that secures you a place in the afterlife.

"Well, at a certain point after my mother died, my dad—still with the Baptist religion—met a certain lady in the church, and they decided they wanted to get married. The minister told my dad that he could not marry them, because she was a divorcée.

"So, all of a sudden, we're no longer Baptists. This lady that my dad decided he wanted to marry is divorced, and the Baptist religion doesn't believe in divorce—or at least that particular version of Baptist that my dad had been participating in—so they couldn't get married in that church. So, all of a sudden, Dad becomes Presbyterian. And Presbyterian is now the way.

"When we were Baptists, everyone else was wrong and they were all going to hell. The next-door neighbors are Catholic, and my dad, as a Baptist, his position was that the Catholic religion was the world's largest cult because they pray to the statue of Mary. These people were absolutely phenomenal, wonderful people. The mom was a godsend. And it was very contradictory to me that somehow these people are bad. Baptist is the right way, so these people are flawed.

"And now, we're no longer Baptists. We're Presbyterian. What just happened?"

This upheaval opened young Dyer's eyes to new possibilities and discoveries. As he got older, studied more, and had new experiences, he began to see what he calls "overlap" between any number of religious beliefs and outlooks on life.

"I began to try and understand the ideas of various religions. I went to a Sikh temple with an Indian friend of mine, and there was a lot of stuff that I didn't understand, but there was a lot of stuff that I said, 'Wow, that was the same stuff that they talk about over there.'

"I went to Catholic church with our next-door neighbors. And there's a lot of overlap there. As I got older, I started looking at all this overlap, and a lot of societal control. I took a couple of philosophy classes, and I read some different guys, and then I took a logic class—and that really screwed my head up. Trying to equate philosophical understandings into mathematical calculations is out of control."

Dyer says that now he does not attend church and considers himself neither Catholic nor Protestant. He has little use for organized religion of any kind, but he does believe in God. Heaven and hell are another matter, and not something with which he concerns himself. "I have to believe—in theory—that we have some kind of supreme power. Because that means there is some kind of penalty, or not penalty. That is the construct that keeps us from just living in anarchy. I'm in a society. I am a member of society and I am participating, and I don't want anarchy. We have to have norms, and we have to have mores. We have to have boundaries. Why do we need societal boundaries? Well, it's to keep people from doing things to other people that they don't want done to them.

"And when people exceed those boundaries, those fences that we put up, then we hold those people accountable. Then we say we do that because God said so. OK, so for the construct of society, I believe that there is a higher power. I don't have a name for him.

"The use of organized religion . . . I'm really happy that it's there, and it made my wife happy to get married in a Methodist church, and I have done work with the United Methodist Church with some fundraisers and stuff that they have done, but I can be happy and not do that. So I choose not to attend.

"To me, it comes down to two possible outcomes: there is fate and predestination, or there is chance and choice. So, under some ideology—like some of the ideas of Protestantism—the idea that there is God and he knows everything that is going to happen, and he says we have free will. But, if he knows what's going to happen, how is that free will? We have the ability to choose, but if he knows what we're going to choose, is it really a choice?

"I believe that life is a series of choices. We have to have control over what we do and who we are. If we don't have control—if everything is fate and predestination—then that eliminates the ability to impact what is going to happen. And that means there is no hope.

"I have to have hope. Not hope of anything in particular. I have to have hope, though. I have to have hope of tomorrow, of [a] future.

"Am I concerned with heaven and hell? I think if I worry about that, it's going to interrupt my ability to proceed through life and be happy. John Lennon said, 'Life is what happens to you when you're busy making other plans.' I think that's a really interesting quote. We can become self-absorbed and distracted, and just balled up in stuff, and for what? What does that mean? What does that get us? And in some people, they're just distracting themselves so that they can get through life. And it's a process of maintaining their distraction, because if they think about actual life, then that becomes tumultuous and unsettling. And I think a number of those people are the most [zealous] of people.

"So, I have no control over the reality or existence of the afterlife. There's some religions that say you need to do this or do that. Depending on which group you read or listen to, you can get all kinds of different how-tos. You know—step one, two, three, this is how you get to heaven. I still have to get from A to B. And I can control that, because I have the ability to choose. And what I choose is happiness."

Chapter 27:

Michele Watson

"In my old belief system, I would have feared death. Now . . . I do not fear death and do not see it as the end of the soul."

She finally met the love of her life at age forty-five, but one year and one week later, the man she describes as her soul mate died from cancer and left Tennessee native Michele Watson questioning just about everything she ever learned about God and death and dying.

"It was two months ago that he passed, and my heart is broken," Watson said, the day after Christmas. "We were highly compatible, best friends, and old souls. He told me I was everything to him; he was everything to me. My life is changed forever by his death.

"It has made me question so much. We both finally found love . . . never really having it prior in our other relationships. Then it is stripped from both of us. My outlook on many things I know is changed forever now.

"Since my husband's death and losing others, it has changed me spiritually. It has made me realize that I have to take off the blinders about God being this great being, or this being that makes me pay for things, or else I might as well not have a [belief] in God at all. I have started looking more at reincarnation because it is the only thing that makes sense for me. Sometimes I feel like I have had so many losses that it has to be karma—not to make me pay for things I have done wrong, but so that I can learn different lessons. So I opened my mind a little more toward reincarnation, since I have always thought it a possibility. Reincarnation may be a lifeboat for me in my spirituality due to those losses, if that makes sense."

Watson, now forty-six, grew up in northeastern Tennessee with a brother, a sister, and a half-sister, and was exposed to a wide variety of different religions as a young girl. She was raised in a Protestant Christian church, the religion of her father. Her mother was raised a Baptist, while her brother was Methodist and her sister agnostic. Her maternal grandmother was Freewill Baptist, and she had friends who were Jehovah's Witness, Catholic, Church of God, Buddhist, New Age, Metaphysical, New Age Christian, and Native American Christian.

"My mother was very open about letting me choose which one was right for me, so it opened me up to many different experiences," she says. "I actually carry a little from all of them with me."

Watson says she inherited a strong sense of intuition from her grandmother and began having dreams of reincarnation and "déjà vu experiences" as a teenager. Those experiences and others opened her eyes to the possibility of such things as reincarnation and past lives.

"I think what happens after we die depends on how it (death) happens. If we feel earthbound through trauma, etc., then I feel our souls stay here for a while until we make our way to heaven. If we have committed suicide or done harm to another, I believe our souls remain at a lower level until we learn certain lessons to help us get toward heaven.

"I believe in a hell as a separation from God and other souls . . . a lonely place. Otherwise, I believe we leave our bodies, meet with our soul group and angels to assist our transition, and later meet with God/Jesus for a life review, without judgment, but simply with instruction to tell us how we could have handled our life situations better. I believe we are given the choice of when we may enter the physical plane again, if we choose. Then with

God, spirit guides, angels, and our soul group, we decide on what lessons will be best and what relationships within that soul group will be best for those who choose to reincarnate again.

"I believe God is a balance of female and male energy, and that God created the world . . . not so much to be a creator, but to be an observer and allow us the free will to create. I believe God is unconditional love, friendship, guidance, mentor, teacher.

"I believe in heaven, and I believe in hell for those who create it for themselves. We can create our own death scenario out of fears that existed prior to death. I believe there is a form of hell—separation from God, loneliness, isolation—where we learn harder lessons than on the other planes. But I do not believe in a fire and brimstone hell.

"I think about dying, but I am not afraid to die. I once heard someone answer the question about being afraid of dying: 'I am not afraid to die—I just don't want to be there when it happens.' I think most people think like that, myself included.

"During my life, I have had many losses. In my old belief system, I would have feared death. Now that I have heard so many stories of reincarnation experiences, I do not fear death and do not see it as the end of the soul. I believe the soul is eternal and that the body dies, not the soul. My husband was the love of my life, so I will not fear the day I can be reunited with him."

Watson, a receptionist who is certified in bookkeeping and data entry, met Joe at work. Their first date was in October 2013, she says, and two months later, they were in love.

"He had bad marriages prior to our meeting one another. I had never been married, and my relationships with my exes were good, but not compatible. I am still good friends with my exes. He was with someone at the time, and I could not interfere with that. It was a long distance relationship that was going nowhere for both of them, so they broke up.

"Then, a friend of ours got us together one night via Facebook. I was scared . . . not sure if he would like me and so on. He told me he loved me in December. He got me a beautiful necklace. In February, I asked his intentions toward me. He thought I was pushing him. I told him I wasn't. He asked me why I was asking. I told him I was afraid he was going to die with cancer before we could legally be married. (He was a smoker.)

"In July, his mom passed on the eleventh, the day we were to leave for a trip we never got to take. In late July, he found out he had cancer.

"It spread quickly. While we were waiting for test results, he asked me for an engagement. He wanted us to have a Confederate wedding and had it all planned. A few days prior to his passing, someone offered to religiously, not legally, marry us. Joe said, 'Let's do it.' I said, 'Absolutely.' We were married in the hospital by an ordained minister—not legally married, because it would affect his insurance and leave me with his health debt.

"It was the night before the morning Joe passed. I got some wooden flowers wrapped in a scarf down at the hospital gift shop, and a shawl at the gift shop. The person who married us brought sparkling grape juice and some plastic cups. We were married. I asked Joe afterward if he was happy and he said, 'Very happy.' So was I. We were married that night, and then the next morning (within 6 hours) he died.

"We were very much in love . . . deeply in love. He told me I was the love of his life. He was the love of my life, my soul mate, and it took me to the age of forty-five to find him and then I lost him.

"I was a new wife and a widow within six hours."

Watson, who does not have children, attends a Protestant Christian church with her mother, and even sings in the choir, but considers herself more a spiritual person than a religious person. "Religion is dogma and a set of rules that no one can ever hope to follow," she says.

She believes in prayer, "talking to God," but thinks meditation, "listening to God," is more important. The meaning of life for her centers around love.

"We are all here to form a community with one another through love and service to each other, and to learn lessons of patience, forgiveness, love, tolerance, and gratitude."

Chapter 28:

Janet Schwind

> *"I don't think about dying. When I die, I gain heaven."*

She went to Catholic Church as a young girl but did not pay much attention or take it too seriously, eventually skipping services altogether to go to a nearby shopping mall with her little brother. It wasn't until years later that Indiana native Janet Schwind faced a personal crisis that led to a life-changing transformation of faith.

"I went to church because my mom made us go," Schwind recalls. "My little brother and I would go on Sundays (mom often went on Saturday night), and we would sit in the balcony and goof off. Eventually, we just skipped church and went to the mall across the street. We'd grab a church bulletin and bring it home to prove to mom that we were at church. I think she probably was on to our scam.

"I went to Catholic grade school through eighth grade. I used to try to listen to sermons when I was younger, and I do believe that I absorbed who God is, enough that I believed he existed. Some messages sank in and helped me to think about the right things. But I didn't go much farther than that with my faith. I was away from God and the church till age thirty-six, when at a particularly difficult point in my life, I sought him out and went back to church, where I encountered Jesus in a vision. This is when my faith transformed.

"It has been an evolving process of discovering more and more about him as I seek him in deeper ways. But the pivotal moment that took me from just believing he existed to actually experiencing him as alive and real was when I was thirty-six. I was in a very difficult emotional place in my life, struggling with something that I couldn't fix. I was in turmoil and actually said out loud, 'I will never be happy again.'

"Around this time, I had been looking to go back to church because I'd been invited to church with a friend on Easter Sunday, and I had an experience there where God just touched my heart. I felt him, and I wanted more. So I finally found a church for myself. During a service, I saw a vision of Jesus on the cross and he was alive still. It was just a brief vision, but in one moment I went from just believing a story in the Bible to actually knowing he is alive. I told him I was sorry for being indifferent to him all my life, and asked him to come and live in my heart. And he did, just because I invited him."

Schwind, who was born in Mishawaka, Indiana, and grew up in South Bend with three brothers and two sisters, has a bachelor's degree in journalism and English from Indiana University Bloomington. A talented and creative artist and painter, she worked for many years as an advertising copywriter and producer, and now freelances as an editor and publishing consultant. She is single and the proud aunt to a dozen nieces and nephews.

Since her remarkable spiritual experience, she has continued to pursue and grow in her faith. She now attends a nondenominational Christian church and follows the teachings of the Bible.

"I do go to church. I attend a church that follows Jesus and believes in the miracles, signs, and wonders of the Holy Spirit, like what Jesus and his disciples did in the Bible.

"I go because I want to be in an environment where I am serving people, helping them find their own relationship with Jesus, and to be around people who will also help me grow in my relationship, and grow in love.

"I consider myself spiritual because I have a spirit. My spirit is what is alive and in relationship with God, and it is the 'me' that will continue to live beyond this natural life. To me, it means living from my spirit, in communion with God's spirit—to do this more and more. It means not living to build my own kingdom but living from God's kingdom, from that identity as his daughter.

"When my dad died when I was twenty-two, I accepted it just because I am a realist, and I know that death is a part of life. I had always thought my dad was kind of amazing, that he was really smart and could do anything . . . and even though we were never super 'close,' I knew he loved me, and he was my sense of security in the world. But when he died, I made an internal vow: I vowed that I would never rely on someone else ever again, that I would be independent and take care of myself.

"Many years later in my adult life, I would repent of this vow and allow God to be my security. He never meant for me to be independent of him. This has been my biggest challenge—to trust God for everything and not try to control it all myself. I suspect this is similar for a lot of people, because many of us grow up thinking we are alone."

As for what happens after we die, Schwind says she believes people will stand for judgment before God, and the final destination then is either heaven or hell. And where we wind up is based on our choices in life.

"I believe in life after death," the fifty-two-year-old says. "The reason that I do is because I believe the word of God, which says that we have been given eternal life in Jesus Christ. I believe God has set eternity in our hearts. We don't always 'feel' that truth, but faith is not about feeling something; it is simply about believing and walking in it.

"I do believe there is a heaven and a hell. I am not completely sure of what both mean, or what they will physically look like. But I am convinced that hell is a place of separation from God, one that is by our own choice. And a place of great regret. Heaven is being with Jesus and God and living in his presence and enjoying him forever.

"There are theories of this, and one is that heaven is actually here. I don't know, really. I don't try to figure out those kinds of things because those mysteries are too great for me to know. What are they? How do we humans get there? Again I believe we 'get' to heaven or hell by our own choice. We either choose God or we choose not to love him. He would love to be chosen. He gives us the choice. He doesn't want puppets. He lets us be free. He loves us either way. But we get what we choose. I think people would like to not accept that responsibility that the choice is up to them, so they come up with their own explanation of heaven and hell that they are comfortable with, one that puts them in a role of 'victim' of God's horrible control. That isn't true about God, though.

"I think it's gonna be mind-blowingly amazing and to try to describe it just wouldn't be possible. But I feel we will be constantly amazed and in awe. And there won't be a sun because there is no need for it—God is light and he will illuminate heaven."

Although she's not ready to go anytime soon, the thought of dying doesn't bother Schwind because she believes she knows what happens after that. In the meantime, she will continue to strive to become the person she thinks she was born to be.

"The purpose of life is to learn how to love, to allow God to continually transform me into the image of his son, Jesus, more and more. To truly live from the identity of the daughter of God that I am. And to commit myself to putting to death all the lies that prevent me from living in this truth.

"I pray because it's how I can have a relationship with God. You can't really be friends with someone you are not talking to. I pray because our prayers are powerful. I pray because I need God as my friend. And because we all need him to move in our lives. I feel closer to him when I pray and can be myself with him. He already knows me better than I know myself. But when I can talk to him about the ugly stuff—my pain and my sadness and my sins—he accepts those prayers as a sacrifice, and he burns them up and fills me up again with his love. That's what brings His heart and mine back together. When I don't pray and don't come to him, it creates a distance from Him that is very cold and empty. He is always there waiting for me to come back. At every moment.

"I don't think about dying. It doesn't scare me at all. When I die, I gain heaven. Occasionally, I think about how awesome it will be to be in a place of total love and peace, and to see God in his fullness, and no more pain, and joy never-ending, and seeing my dad again, and my grandparents (and getting to actually have a conversation with my mom's parents—they were Italian and spoke no English, and I never understood them!), and my beloved doggie, Nick.

"I believe we will be immediately present with the Lord, as it says in the word of God. I think there is a time of 'judgment,' where God looks at our hearts to see if we knew him. I think only God knows what's in each person's heart

"I believe in him because I am in a relationship with him. He has shown himself to me in many ways throughout my life and our relationship continues to grow and transform as I seek him more deeply. We are in collaboration on my life.

"I feel a sense of relief that he exists and is the Creator of all things, and has the greatest power over all things and all the answers—and that he is *good*. I like to read the book of Isaiah to be reminded of his power and majesty and might. And then I think, 'And *that's* my dad.'"

Chapter 29:

Amanda Sanchez

> *"It's just a transition. We get out of these sick bodies and our soul doesn't feel pain anymore."*

When her father died ten years ago from liver cancer, Amanda Sanchez was heartbroken, but then he appeared to her in a dream, and that visit convinced the El Salvador native that life after death is very real and also that death is not something to be feared.

"I loved him so much," Sanchez, sixty-seven, says.

"I was in a lot of grief, but one night I had a very vivid dream about him. I dreamed he appeared to me and he was very happy, and he touched the side where he used to hurt so much, and he said to me, 'Look, it doesn't hurt anymore,' and he smiled. It had a profound effect on me."

Although she and her sister went to a Catholic church when she was a child growing up in Central America, she no longer considers herself to be religious, but rather more spiritual in her belief system. She believes in a supreme being she refers to as God and also believes there is a heaven, but not a hell. Her idea of life after death involves the idea of reincarnation, learning lessons, and overcoming past mistakes.

"When I was a little girl, my mother brought us up going to church, but not faithfully. I did do my first communion and after that we didn't go to church that much. I was about ten years old and then my parents stopped taking us. No special reason . . . only that my father was not happy with the Catholic religion.

"We stopped going until I was fourteen, then my parents converted to the Lutheran Church, and we used to go faithfully to church. I did love that church, but I grew up, got married at twenty-one, and didn't go to church any more. When I had my kids (two boys), I enrolled my first kid in a Catholic school, and my second went to the same school, but only one year after that, I never went to church again.

"Later in life, I grew very curious and wanted to know which was the right religion. I informed myself, read books, researched a lot, and came to my own conclusion. I think it doesn't matter what religion you follow; it is the belief in a supreme being and to understand the rules we are supposed to follow that is important.

"I don't follow the Bible to a tee. I believe God is all about love and forgiveness, and I don't believe in hell.

"I don't go to church, but I believe I can talk to God anywhere and at any time. I pray because I do believe in a supreme being, and mostly I pray to thank him for everything I have, and to guide me in my life to make the right decisions and help people who need help."

When a person dies, Sanchez says, the soul leaves the body and travels toward "a light," where it is met by spirit guides who lead the way to God.

"I believe we meet with that supreme being, and he goes through our entire life, where we see the good and bad we did while we were still alive, and the consequences our actions caused to our fellow men.

"I did a lot of research, and I always was a very spiritual person since I was a kid, and inside of me, I feel I am in the right path," says Sanchez, a vocational assistant for the blind for twenty-three years who now lives in New Jersey.

"I think we lived before and we made mistakes, and we come back to try to fix our mistakes of the previous life . . . to improve ourselves and become better souls, and eventually when we reach that point, we won't come back anymore. Also, we come here with a mission, and until we accomplish this mission, we can't leave this world.

"So dying, I think it's not a big deal. I am not afraid. Sooner or later, we all have to die. It's just a transition. We get out of these sick bodies and our soul doesn't feel pain anymore."

Chapter 30:

Nabeel Sakhnini

> *"Once I made that commitment to make Jesus my Lord and Savior, I no longer fear death. Not at all."*

As his younger brother lay dying of liver disease and related complications, Nabeel "Bill" Sakhnini saw a peacefulness cross the suffering man's countenance that reinforced even further his already concrete belief in divinity and in life after death.

"That's the beauty of being a believer," said Sakhnini, who was born and raised in Nazareth, Israel. "My brother was a believer, and as he was taking his last few breaths, you could see that he had peace. The peace that passes all understanding. He had that peace, because even though he kind of knew he was taking his last breaths, he knew where he was going."

Sakhnini, fity-seven, grew up in a Christian family, the son of an Israeli Arab Baptist preacher. After graduating from high school, he came to the United States to attend college on a partial scholarship at Gardner-Webb University in Boiling Springs, North Carolina, graduating in 1978 with a biology degree. He then joined the US Army, where he spent twenty years before retiring as a sergeant first class in 1997.

It was shortly after graduating from Gardner-Webb that the young Israeli turned his back on his highly disciplined upbringing and decided to sow a few wild oats.

"I was a pretty good kid for the most part, did good in school, never got into any serious trouble.

"Our parents were tough on us back home. Divorce back then did not exist, so every kid had two parents in their home, a mother and a father. And life was difficult, more challenging, just because of the Middle Eastern customs and traditions. You were raised to respect your elders, regardless of who they were. People were allowed—not only your parents, but your relatives, teachers at school, principals—to not just spank you, but to whip you.

"Let's say if I misbehaved at school, regardless of the seriousness of the offense, I received my first whipping/beating at school by the principal and his assistants—not with a switch, but with a board—and then the second punishment was when we got home. We knew we were going to get it from our parents, as well. So we thought about it twice before we acted up at school.

"It's just the way life was. People were much more respectful. We didn't have all the technology and luxury items that we enjoy nowadays. We didn't have a TV, a telephone, a car, growing up. So we played in the streets. Life was totally different.

"I absolutely believe in spare the rod, spoil the child. That's what the word says. The book of Proverbs. I'm a firm believer in that. I raised my kids that way. They knew that when Dad said something, I meant what I said. I spanked them—never out of anger. I've always made sure I took a couple of minutes and kind of cooled off, calmed down, before I got the belt or the switch or whatever I was using.

"Unfortunately, nowadays, people think it's child abuse, and one can easily get in trouble with the law and with social services and so on. And it's definitely not getting any better.

"So I was always a good kid, and then pretty much after college, I would say, things changed," he said, smiling and chuckling. "I graduated in 1978—I was only twenty when I graduated—and I just wanted to see what it was like. I was doing a lot of crazy things. Drinking and just living in the clubs, so on and so forth. I've never done drugs, thank God. I've seen what drugs did to some of my first cousins and other relatives, and so I was always scared of drugs."

He joined the army in 1981 and continued his hell-raising ways for a number of years, until a friend convinced him to go to church. Eventually, he felt moved by what he heard there, and he said a prayer and asked God to change his life.

"Once I made that commitment and let God into my life—back into my life—the Bible says he will make a new creature out of the sinner, the person. The desire to drink was no longer there. It was sudden, and it was quick.

"I was a very heavy drinker for a couple, three years. I had a very volatile temper and a foul mouth. I'd probably be in jail or dead now if I hadn't made that commitment. Yes, sir. But God snatched all that away from me in the blink of an eye. The spirit of God can move in miraculous ways, and once he starts talking to your heart, it's basically over.

"I became a totally different person. I was stationed at Fort Dix, New Jersey, and my wife was visiting my in-laws in Texas for Christmas. We were helping deploy the National Guard and Reserves to Bosnia. None of us who were assigned to that unit could take leave or anything, so when I finally caught up with her maybe three or four weeks later, she could not believe it was the same person.

"I had started bowing my head, praying over my meal, thanking God for it, that sort of thing. And life has been good since.

"It's taken me years to get to this point, to become the person I've become over the past fifteen, twenty years. It's all because of God's grace. I spend a lot of time in prayer, a lot of time in the word, because the Bible says that many believers, many people, perish because of a lack of knowledge. It's important. The Bible is our daily bread. We nourish our bodies physically, and the word of God is our spiritual nourishment. If we don't read it on a daily basis, our spirit will not grow, and we will not get the knowledge we need to become the people God has created us to become.

"So it's important that we read the word on a daily basis. That way, when a storm comes our way, I know what to do, what to say. I don't react, I act, according to the word of God. Because I have the knowledge to make it through the storm. This is where a lot of people fail, if you will. A storm comes and they are devastated, overwhelmed, depressed, because they have no clue what God's word says.

"I'm a happy person with a genuine smile on my face. Not only am I blessed, God uses me to be a blessing to many others. I'm very thankful, and I'm grateful."

Sakhnini is now a public school teacher, divorced once and married to his new wife, Angela, for twenty-one years, the proud father of five children, and grandfather to five more. He is a dedicated churchgoer and student of the Bible who attends and often leads regular study classes, at his home and elsewhere.

As a devout Christian, he believes unwaveringly in such things as life after death, heaven and hell, sin and salvation, and the Bible story of Jesus Christ. Because of all that, he says he has no fear of death whatsoever. He was created for a purpose, and when he has fulfilled that purpose, he will then be called to meet his maker.

"Before I made that commitment and let the Lord into my life and turned my life—completely—over to him, the only thing I feared was death. Because I had no clue which way I would go. I was doing a lot of crazy things.

"That's the only thing I feared back then, was dying. I came close more than once, but I believe it was my parents' prayers for me, interceding on my behalf, is what saved my life. And once I made that commitment to make Jesus my Lord and Savior, I no longer fear death. Not at all.

"Yes, we're going to die one day. But our spirit will continue to live on.

"The Bible—the word of God—is my main reference, and I can start with probably the most popular scripture in the Bible. That is John 3:16, which says, 'For God so loved the world that he gave his only begotten son, that whoever believes in him will not perish, but have eternal life.'

"That verse alone tells me that there is life after death. God created us in his image, according to the book of Genesis. God is a spirit, so we are a spirit. We have a soul that comprises our intellect, our emotions, our mind, and we live in this physical body. And the spirit that God has created never dies.

"The story of the crucifixion, mentioned throughout the four Gospels. I'll go with one scripture from the book of Luke, chapter twenty-three, verse forty-three, when the criminal on the other side of Jesus repented on the cross, and Jesus looked toward him and said, 'Assuredly, I say to you today you will be with me in paradise.' That's another confirmation that life was not going to end for the criminal on the cross, that day when he took his last breath.

"Other scriptures that confirm life after death—John 11:25. Jesus is speaking to a woman, and he says to her, 'I am the resurrection and the life. He who believes in me, though he may die, he shall live.'

"I'm a firm believer [that] there's got to be life after this life here. Our spirit never dies. When our spirit leaves planet Earth, we go straight to heaven to be with the Lord."

Whether we stay in heaven, according to Sakhnini, depends on our beliefs here in Earth. There is only one way to get there and be invited through the gates, he says, and unfortunately, not everyone will receive the invitation.

"There are no second chances at all. What the Bible says also is that those who believe will not be judged. Anybody who is not a believer, the wrath of God is going to be overwhelming, very severe, and it's going to catch a lot of people by surprise.

"The Bible clearly says Jesus is the son of God and our Lord. He said, 'I am the way, the truth and the life. No one can get to the father except through me.' So he is the only way. Not the Virgin Mary, not Buddha, not Mohammed. Jesus is the only way to go to Father God.

"The Bible clearly states that our good works are like filthy rags before the Lord. So regardless of how many good deeds we accomplish on planet Earth, how many good things we do, how many people we help, that by itself is not enough. Sure, all those things are great and we all need to be doing these things . . . however, none of these things will get us to heaven. The only way to heaven is through salvation by believing in Jesus Christ as the son of God, as the Lord and Savior.

"We have to be prepared to meet our maker. Tomorrow is not guaranteed for anyone. I could be driving home this afternoon and [he snaps his fingers] just like that, I'm gone. That's why I encourage people not to wait. The word says, 'Today is the day of salvation; today is the day of repentance.' "

Chapter 31:

Barbara S.

> *"I used to think of just lying there, rotting away in the ground. But then I realized the body is only a vessel for your soul and spirit, and once you die, it is released."*

A variety of religious and spiritual influences and explorations throughout her fifty-five years has left Connecticut native Barbara S. convinced that there is some form of life after death, although she no longer believes in the heaven and hell teachings of her youth.

"I just started to think that the church God wasn't how I believed God to be," says Barbara, a single mother of two and thirty-year federal government employee who asked that her real name not be used. "Actually, I was quite lost there for a while and had no faith. Then I went into Wicca for a while, [and] I liked it. It dealt with worshipping the Mother Earth. I stayed there quite awhile.

"Then, I evolved into just doing my own thing, as far as religion and what I believe, and I raised my daughters the same way. And now they are young adults, and they are happy in what they believe to be so—for themselves, religion-wise.

"I believe the universe is God. I think of everything there is in the world as God/universe. I believe our soul goes to a place where we see a remake of our life and all the things we did wrong and right. I believe you come back and reincarnate, to try to right the wrongs—hence your karma.

"I believe you create your own hell or heaven. I don't really believe it is a place.

"I believe you do see other souls that have passed away in your lifetime, and if you were unkind to them, then that is the time you face your maker, so to speak. I believe you learn lessons from people, and once you learned the lesson, then you move on to other people; but if you didn't learn the lesson, then you face them again in another lifetime, and it keeps going until you finally learn the lesson, and then you move up in your wisdom."

Barbara grew up the middle child in a family of three girls, in a home that she says was not particularly religious. They went to a nearby Catholic church on Easter and Christmas, but that was about it.

"We had our baptism, and Holy Communion, and confirmation, but we never actually talked about God or anything spiritual in our house when I was a kid. I think my mother was more religious when she was younger. She grew up in a small village, and the Church was the social center. But for our own upbringing, no. I always thought of God as the big man up in the sky with the beard looking down on what I was doing.

"When I had my daughters, I did the same exact thing my parents did to me as far as church. Only went on Easter and Christmas. Now, I regret it. I wish I had brought my daughters more—not for the religion, but for the community spirit, the feeling of belonging to something.

"I was in church one day, and the priest was giving a sermon. It was during the *Roe v, Wade* controversy. The priest was going on about abortion, and there was this little girl standing next to me, and she turned and asked her mom what did abortion mean. I could see the mom was perplexed, to say the least, on how to answer her daughter. I thought to myself, 'I didn't come here to hear this abortion stuff. I could put the news on the television for that.' And that was the last time I attended church.

"Catholics also believe that they were born into sin, and you have to ask God for forgiveness of those sins. I don't believe that; I don't believe an innocent baby just born already has a sin. I don't believe you have to ask God for forgiveness of your sins; you have to forgive yourself."

Now she considers herself a spiritual person and believes in the power of prayer. No one close to her has died, but she probably was most affected by the death of her ex-husband, her daughter's dad.

"My parents are still alive, and my ex-husband and I were divorced for a long time before he passed away. He had a heart attack, so it was unexpected and sudden. It made me realize that you just never know—here today and gone tomorrow. It made me think about life, regrets, etc. Plus, there was the sorrow and complete helplessness of me trying to help my daughters through their grief.

"I don't think about my own death because it would make me sad. I try not to think of how many years I might have left. I am fifty-five years old, so half my life has passed. I am not afraid. I used to be afraid of it. I used to think of just lying there rotting away in the ground. But then I realized the body is only a vessel for your soul and spirit, and once you die, it is released.

"I believe you come here to carry out a plan for yourself, a mission. And that is where you will find your joy and passion. The trouble is, trying to figure out exactly what it is you are here to do. Some people know right away. People that want to be doctors, or engineers, or artists from the get-go, while others struggle with finding their true purpose. So I believe if you didn't find it the first time around, then you come back again, until you fulfill your life purpose.

"I believe in taking care of the Earth and all living things. I am a tree hugger. I believe in fairies and angels and ghosts. Religious, to me, means going to church, behaving a certain way, not leaving the box, so to say. Strict rules.

"I believe in the power of prayer. I believe that when you pray, you are baring your soul, and I believe when you believe in the power of your prayer, that's when it will be answered."

Chapter 32:

Whit Crandall

"I'm not too sure what happens after we die."

Lubbock, Texas native Whit Crandall says he thinks about dying now and then, but the idea does not bother him much because he has been there before.

"I've died from overdoses more than once," the burly fifty-eight-year-old biker and man of very few words, says. "I think about dying sometimes, but no, I'm not afraid of it. It's a way to get to where we all want to be."

Crandall, who is divorced with three sons, has worked as a house painter for thirteen years and a mental health technician for five years. He graduated from high school in Houston in 1974 and has two brothers.

Growing up and throughout most of his life, Crandall never went to church, and he still is not a big fan, but he started attending some services recently, more out of curiosity than anything else.

"When I was growing up, we didn't go to church as a family. I was given my own way to figure out my path.

"I've always believed in a higher power, even in my [drug] addiction. When I think of God, I think of an old man with a beard, with angels by his side. And, yes, I believe in heaven and hell. If you believe in one, you had better know they both exist.

Where or what they are, I don't know, but I think we get to either by our actions here in this reality."

He believes in life after death and considers himself more a spiritual person than a religious one.

"I don't believe that going to 'church' will get you anywhere," Crandall says. "But I've started to go with my girlfriend, and wanted to see for myself what I'd been missing. I pray a lot because it's part of the [recovery] program. I'm not sure what happens after we die, but I've heard enough about it (life after death) to believe that I would rather be right and not wrong about there being an afterlife."

Chapter 33:

Nancy Harvey

"I believe that as soon as you die, you either go to heaven or you go to hell."

Dying is not something she thinks too much about, but South Korea native Nancy Harvey says she knows exactly what is going to happen.

"I do believe in life after death. I believe that as soon as you die, you either go to heaven or you go to hell," says Mrs. Harvey, a thirty-year-old mother of three boys.

"I don't believe in a purgatory or anything like that. I believe there is a Judgment Day. I believe everybody, as soon as they die, is going to face God and—I don't know exactly how it would go—receive judgment, not based off of your works but whether you accepted Jesus Christ as your savior. You're either going to be allowed into heaven or you're going to hell.

"One of the things that my church teaches is that is why it is very important to do missionary work. To reach out to people—in other countries, for example—who have never had the chance to hear the truth about Jesus. I think it would be nice if there were more than one way to get to heaven. I think that would allow more people to get in. But do I believe that? No. Jesus is the only way."

Mrs. Harvey was born in Seoul to a Korean mother and US Army soldier father. She lived there the first two years of her life, then spent another two years in Germany before moving permanently to the United States.

Religion did not play a big part in her life until she was a teenager. Her parents divorced when she was eight, her mother never cared much for organized religion, and so the family did not belong to a church. That changed—temporarily—when young Nancy was a teenager.

"I don't know what her background is, as far as religion, but my mom is very against church, in general. The reason she gives is the fact they are 'always asking for money.' That really irks her.

"I think that probably comes from struggling financially. She is very protective of her money, so she's very against donating. She grew up poor, then when she divorced my father, she had to raise me and my sister as a single mom for a few years. She's just struggled a lot.

"My first experience going to church was when I was thirteen years old. One of her Korean friends was always inviting my mom to church, but she would never go. So her friend invited me and my sister, and I started going to Northside Baptist Church with them. I had only gone there for maybe two months before I got saved. Pretty much immediately after that happened, my mom told me that I couldn't go anymore.

"So as a very new Christian, I was yanked right back out of church and fell right back into living a worldly life. It was frustrating and hurtful because I knew she didn't have any good reason really to do that. She didn't understand religious reasons for wanting to go, so she couldn't sympathize or empathize with me on my arguments for why I should go. She didn't get it, so she didn't care.

"The reasoning she gave was that there were some teenage boys that went to that church, and I guess it was reported that I was speaking to them, and her impression was that I was going to church only for that reason—for boys. So to keep me away from that, she told me to stop. It really was not the reason or purpose, but... and it ended up that one of the guys I was friends with, I later married, and he is now my husband (Daniel)."

151 | *Chapter 33: Nancy Harvey*

Her mother has always been a strong influence in her life, Mrs. Harvey says, and not necessarily in a good way. Her mom has been married several times and holds strong opinions about a lot of things with which she simply does not agree.

She moved in with Daniel immediately upon leaving her mother's home, and a few months later, they got married. Her mom did not attend the wedding.

"We had a marriage at the church, but she didn't come. I knew she wasn't going to come, and I know that even if she did come, she wouldn't be supportive, so it didn't really hurt my feelings that she wasn't there. What really bothered me was that I wanted my sister there, and she wouldn't let her come.

"We didn't talk for a long time, but within a year of me getting married, I got pregnant, and as soon as I got pregnant, that was a whole 'nuther level of rift between us.

"Now, when my first son was born, she saw him and instantly fell in love. So that kind of helped with our relationship, but it hasn't been totally mended.

"It's a touchy relationship. I feel like I have to be very patient with her, so it can be frustrating.

"We just kind of take it one day at a time. We have a good relationship, I guess you could say, whenever we do speak to each other. We're civil and we get along, but it's when she says or does things that I don't agree with, it frustrates me. I think she has shown me—I hate to say this; it's so sad to say this—but she has shown me what I don't want to be. She's shown me how not to act, how not to be.

"I think it would be very difficult for me and her to make true amends at this point, because we would have to work through some things, and I don't think there is a compromise we could come to."

While she has firm beliefs in such things as God, Jesus, heaven and hell, the afterlife, and so on, Mrs. Harvey admits that she falls short in a number of areas. After returning to active churchgoing at age eighteen, she has "backslid" in recent years and no longer attends church very often. She feels guilty about that sometimes, but she does not think church attendance or the lack thereof has any effect on her salvation.

"It's very easy to get backslid, and it's very hard to get back into the swing of things. When I'm in church, I'm very happy, and I know that's where I should be. But the second I leave, and I'm back in the world, it's like it all goes down the drain. It's very hard to stay committed. I guess if I made the decision to surround myself with other Christians, they would encourage me and things like that.

"I was never exposed to anything religious until I started going to that church when I was a kid. And I pretty much accepted it immediately. I don't know if I had gone to a different church that believed completely differently if I would have grasped onto that just as easily or quickly. I don't know. Maybe that just ended up being the way it worked out. Maybe I was wanting that so much that I immediately latched onto it. I don't know.

"It gives me a security. I believe the Bible to be 100 percent literal truth—the word of God—and I feel that I'm 100 percent correct in my beliefs. But you would think that if somebody is that strict, I guess, in what they believe, that it would affect the way they live their life. And like I said, I've been in and out of church since I was eighteen. I'm thirty now, so . . . right now, I'm probably more out than in.

"So the way that I live my life, I don't think other people would be able to see that in me. Because I'm that much backslid at this point, but that does not mean that I don't believe, or that what I believe is wrong. Am I doing the right thing? No. But I still have the same basic beliefs.

"I would like to think that it guides my daily decisions, but like I said, I make those decisions on a daily basis, and I don't always choose to do the right things. But I think it largely guides how I raise my children, because I want them to have that assurance of going to heaven, as well."

As far as the purpose or meaning of life, Mrs. Harvey says that the God she believes in has a purpose for everyone, and it is up to the individual to find out what that purpose is and then pursue it.

"I think initially, in your primary years, hopefully your parents are raising you in a church or a religious background so that you can eventually be saved. I think that should be the primary goal at first.

"Then, once you are saved and you are growing as a Christian, I think that you need to find out what God has planned for your life and do that, whatever that is. Whether it's missionary work or working at McDonald's. Whatever is his plan for you, I think that should be your goal for the rest of your life. But outside of that, I think every Christian's goal should be to see other saved, or to spread the word."

She prays sometimes, but like her church attendance, it tends to be somewhat sporadic. She thinks about her own death now and then, but it is not something she focuses much energy on, mostly because she believes in her heart that her next destination is heaven.

"I don't worry about it. Does it cross my mind sometimes? Yes. I think about it sometimes, but it's not something that I worry about. Maybe it's because I know I'm saved that I don't worry about it?

"I remember as a teen, or even as a child, thinking about it and being more worried then. Not really knowing or understanding what was going to happen after the fact, but I don't worry about it now. I worry about people I care about that I know are not saved. I worry about them. That bothers me."

Chapter 34:

Tony Barrio

> *"I believe in life after death, in the sense that after you die, there is some energy that escapes, and there is something left behind. Energy does not disappear, and this energy goes in space ... somewhere."*

As a young boy growing up in the Santos Suarez neighborhood in Havana, Cuba, it was an honor when Tony Barrio was chosen to attend the prestigious Belen College, an institute run by the Jesuits and normally reserved primarily for children of the upper class.

Barrio spent more than six years at Belen, undergoing rigorous training and education for the Catholic priesthood, until he decided one day when he was twelve that he'd had enough.

"You are there all the time; you go to school constantly—twelve months a year; eight hours a day. You learn foreign languages, history, geography, everything like that, and then you learn catechism and religion and all that.

"Your family can come see you on weekends, but otherwise you are there. The brainwashing is unbelievable. It was strict. Walk in single file, don't speak, have spiritual exercises. We were unable to speak for seven days at a time. We had to think and write and pray—all that kind of bullshit.

"In the thirties, when I was born, the Jesuits were the dominant force in Cuba. They really ran the country, in the background. When you were in the first to second grade, you had to take certain tests. My brother and I both passed the tests, and we were picked to go to Belen—me first, and he a couple of years later.

"Belen was an institute for the very, very rich. If you are a graduate from Belen, it's like Harvard or Yale. My dad was a bookkeeper, and we were lower middle class. We ate meals, we had shoes, but we were poor.

"Just about everybody became priests. But I somehow had a revelation, and I said, 'To hell with these guys.' I'd see some of them drinking, and see other things, and something told me, 'This is bullshit.' I already had about six or seven years of education with them, and then one day I jumped the fence. I escaped from Belen.

"By then, my parents were getting divorced, and so I stayed with my mother. I told her I didn't want to go back. I was telling her all the things that happened. Then, she got my brother out of there, too."

Four years after leaving Belen, Barrio got a job as a mess boy on a Cuban merchant marine ship. After two years of sailing mostly between Cuba and Spain, his ship headed for the United States, landing at the Domino Sugar Refinery in Brooklyn, New York, and Barrio saw his chance to fulfill a lifelong dream of moving to America.

At age eighteen, he jumped ship, worked as a bus boy for two months at a Central Park restaurant, then headed to Buffalo and got a temporary job as a seaman aboard a Great Lakes tanker ship. He later joined the US military, serving in the air force and the army, and earned his citizenship while stationed in England.

He went on to earn multiple college degrees and became an award-winning polygraph examiner, both in the military and as a civilian.

In spite of all that early religious training—or perhaps because of it—Barrio, now eighty-two, no longer has anything to do with organized religion. He believes in a supreme being, but calls it "great architect of the universe" rather than God.

"Organized religion is crap. Religion is belief—your own belief. I don't believe in any organized religion, and I looked for it later on in life by taking different religion courses. The closest that I could come to was I went to some meetings, and if anybody asked, 'Which one do you consider yourself more associated with?' I would say, 'I am a Messianic Jew.'

"First of all, because the Bible is nothing more than the history of the Jewish people. That's all it is—a history book. They talk about God, but it's the history of the Jewish people.

"That is the one religion that I feel is closest to the truth. We know that Jesus existed. There is proof that he was tried, that he was crucified, that he was taught to say that he was the king of the Jews, that he went to the temple. When you get down to it, it is this: Jesus was a Jew, his parents were Jews, he was raised as a Jew, he was circumcised, he went to the [Jewish] temple, and he called it 'the house of my father.'

"I'm a rational person with a conscious. I know what's right and what's wrong. That is my religion.

"I believe in life after death, in the sense that after you die, there is some energy that escapes, and there is something left behind. Like when you smoke a cigar or burn a piece of wood, something escapes and there is something left. Everything is energy, in my mind. Energy does not disappear, and this energy goes in space . . . somewhere.

"There is nothing like we travel to some particular place, but this energy continues. I don't know what that energy is, but I believe it has something to do with electromagnetism. It is part of the universe; part of the whole system of creation.

"I'm a Mason. In Masonry—which is not a religion, but a fraternity—our goal is to make a good person better. You don't have to believe in God to be a Mason, but you have to believe in some kind of architect of the universe. So I believe that there is a force—a source—that created the universe. We can go back to the Big Bang, to something, and ask, 'Who did that?'

"So I believe there is something, a great architect of the universe. Even if you were to use the Judeo-Christian bible . . . in the beginning, it says, 'God created the heavens and the Earth, and the spirit of God moved upon the surface of the water . . . and God said let there be light.' So on and so on.

"The definition of spirit to me, in my logic and in my thinking and in my years, is energy. Some unseen force. I cannot comprehend that humans are happenstance. That evolution has occurred is obvious. Evolution has occurred out of design, and as a result is inexplicable.

"I believe that it is inexplicable as to what we are—we don't know. The only thing that I feel is that there is some force. I don't think that God is a person. I don't think of God as a human form. I don't think there's a guy over there somewhere, whether his name is God, Jesus, Muhammad, Buddha, or whatever. I don't believe in any of those things.

"But I believe that there is something out there that by design causes things to happen. Something that is inexplicable. Our mind cannot comprehend infinity, and our mind cannot comprehend certain things, like the creation of the Earth. All we have is theories. There is no one that is actually proven. Your theory is as good as mine. I don't care how many degrees in astronomy you might have, or what religion you are, no one can prove what happened."

Heaven and hell, meanwhile, exist here on Earth, inside the hearts and minds of each individual person, according to Barrio. They are not actual places created for eternal reward or punishment.

"If you have ever read Dante's *Inferno*, you hear about the hottest fires in hell. But I don't believe there is a fire and you're burning forever. You are a soul, so what can you feel?

"I don't believe in hell, nor do I believe there is a nirvana, where you're going to go and have these fifty-seven virgins or angels with harps. I don't believe any of that.

"I believe that we have a conscience. And our conscience tells us when we are doing something right or something wrong. Conscience, whether or not it was formed by our parents or our society, whether it was formed by our contacts or our readings, or whatever inspired us, I believe that conscience is an innate part of being a human being. And I think that human beings know when they do something wrong.

"You know when you do something wrong, and that is what I believe is good and evil. And the recompense you get when you do something good—to me, that is heaven. In other words, if I do something that I know is good—and not for selfishness—but it is something that afterward gives you satisfaction, that is heaven.

"When you do something bad—especially if you're a person who has ever taken a life, for some reason—there is a guilt, and to me you are in hell. I don't believe in the resurrection, or that you come back in another life, any of those things.

"Organized religion is the best invention that man ever made. Going to a garage don't make you a mechanic; going to church don't make you a saint. You don't have to go to church. You have your conscience; you know what is right and what is wrong."

As the number of birthdays ahead of him grows increasingly smaller than the ones behind, Barrio thinks more about his own death, but in a practical sort of way, rather than with any kind of trepidation. The father of two, grandfather of one, and great-grandfather of two more, is mostly concerned with what he leaves behind, and that he has provided adequately for his family.

"I'm not in a big hurry—if there's somebody over there with a gun, I'm not going to go over there—but am I afraid that eventually I am going to die? No. I expect it. It's going to happen, and when it comes, it comes. There's no question about it. And I am prepared for it. That's why I have accountants, and I keep a check on my [financial] things.

"I know I'm not going to be here forever, and I'm not afraid of it. My fear is how I die. I just hope that it is a peaceful death, and that it does not happen for a long, long time.

"I just hope that when it comes, it's not painful or anything like that. I'm more afraid of how I'm going to die than of dying. The dying, in itself, is nothing. I expect it. It's going to happen."

Chapter 35:

Susanne Sims

> *"It's an idea that is so huge that we can't comprehend it, and I think it's kind of fun that we get to live in this mystery."*

Regular visits to cemeteries as a child with her parents and her brothers and sisters fostered a lifelong fascination with death and dying for Minnesota native Susanne Sims, who not only believes in an afterlife but has experienced it firsthand.

"I don't believe—I know," Sims says. "I've had enough experiences to say it's a certainty rather than a belief."

A graduate of the University of Minnesota with a degree in journalism, Sims was raised in a devout Catholic home and remembers the family making frequent visits to the graves of relatives on holidays and other special occasions. During one such trip, her younger brother asked a question that set the course for a lifetime of exploration and study for his older sister, Susanne.

"He was only about four or five years old, and he said the most profound thing: 'Mom and Dad, isn't it true that the minute you're born, you start to die?' Out of the mouths of babes, you know?

"My parents tried to answer the best they could, but I think from that moment on, I thought, 'This seems to be a very interesting revolving door here.'

"So, I was always fascinated by the subject of life after death. Are we really alive? Or are we dreaming right now? Is this reality, or is there another reality beyond this?

"In high school—I think it was my senior year—we had a chance to write a report in a psychology class about any subject we wanted to. I chose the subject of death. And that was when Raymond Moody's book, *Life After Life*, had just come out, so I read that book and did my report. From there, I started reading even more books, and I was very fascinated by these things."

Born and raised in the North Star State, also known as the Land of Ten Thousand Lakes, Sims has lived the past thirty years in Hawaii. She has worked in advertising sales, owned her own marketing company, and now feeds her creative soul as a writer, composer, singer, and stage actress.

The fifty-five-year-old has had a number of profound spiritual experiences during her life, including vivid recalls of past lives. It was during her college years that she had a fateful dream involving one of her three sisters.

"We were very close," Sims says. "We were going to college at that time, and we were waitressing at a twenty-four-hour restaurant, so we had these very late shifts that we worked together.

"I went to bed one night, and I had a dream that I died. I saw myself crossing the street, at night, and these headlights came at me, and I was hit by this car. I felt my body kind of roll over onto the hood of the car and into the windshield and then off onto the pavement. The ambulance came to get me, and they started trying to resuscitate me, and I saw myself drifting further and further away from the scene, and then going through these stages that I had been reading about. Going through the tunnel and seeing the light, relatives showing up . . . and all of a sudden, I panicked, and I thought, 'Oh, my God, am I really dying, or is this just a dream?' So I woke up.

"I was really impacted quite deeply by this dream, and that morning I told my sister all about the dream, and all about the books I'd been reading about death, and we talked about our hopes and our fears about everything.

"About this same time, she was moving. She had finished with her schooling and was going to Tucson, Arizona to do her first student teaching. After she left, she died in those very same circumstances—exactly the way that I had seen it in the dream. What I thought had happened to me was what actually happened to her about a month later.

"I did not put two and two together right away because I was in such shock. It was maybe a month or two later that I sat down one day to have a cup of coffee or whatever, and suddenly the penny dropped and I went, 'Wow.' I forgot about that dream and forgot that we'd had all that conversation about everything. From that point on, I was convinced that we live with very limited eyes for seeing what our real state of being is. How there are these two different worlds, and these two worlds always seem to be in touch with each other, even though it seems mysterious to us."

In the years following her sister's tragic death, Sims says they have communicated through use of a Ouija board, although it has been some time since she has attempted to make any contact.

"I got some very interesting messages from her. Eventually, I decided to let that go because I didn't want to disturb her any more.

"If you've ever used a Ouija board, you know that it requires you to go to each letter, to spell out what it is that needs to be said. Well, at one point . . . I thought it was so clever because she was using shorthand. She said, 'Tell Mike'—who was her boyfriend—'xoxoxo.' I thought how clever that was, instead of 'Tell Mike that I love him,' she took the shorthand route.

"She also talked to me about some things that were going on in my life that she was concerned about, and I thought, 'Wow, this is very interesting.' I would never have expected her to be giving me some sisterly advice. Usually, we are trying to get information from that side, but she started asking me about some health issues and other concerns that she knew I had been dealing with.

"My feeling is, she could have reincarnated by now. It's been over twenty years. I really don't know. I think there's so many other possible worlds and universes out there. I don't believe this is the only place and planet where we can experience our consciousness.

"I just don't know. I don't know if she chose to come back to this world—she left at a very young age. She was only twenty-three. She was a very beautiful soul; she worked with special education children. I think she was highly evolved, and maybe she's moved on to some other world. This is not the most evolved or advanced place, by any means."

Another life after death experience occurred much later, when Sims was on a cruise along the Nile River in Egypt. A hypnotherapist was on board the cruise ship, and out of curiosity, she decided to undergo a past-life regression.

She wound up going back in time to the former Yugoslavia, where she was a young man working as a sea merchant, sailing around different parts of the world, married with two children. After coming back from a voyage, she went to some sort of political meeting and was killed.

"I had a wife, and her parents lived with us, and they came down to meet me when I got off the boat, and we went home together in this cute little wagon, with the hay and the whole thing," Sims recalled. "The house was so beautiful, with the fireplace . . . I was so in love with life, so in love with my family and my children.

"Then at night, what happened was I went out to a meeting, apparently a political meeting, and I was one of the spokespeople in that particular village, and I was trying to represent the serfs and the people who were working the land and not being treated fairly. We were asking for more—people were starving; they were not getting enough percentage of the crops—and our concerns were not being addressed.

"Then, these military guards showed up, and they wanted to make an example of me, so they pushed me around and bullied me, and before I knew it, I was on the ground and a big boulder was thrown at my chest. They killed me.

"I remember while I was having this past life regression, I thought, 'Oh, my God, my chest hurts.' I could feel physically that pain again, and it really, really hurt. I was very concerned for my family, because I thought they were going to harm them. So, I'm in this after-death state, and I decided I wasn't going to go anywhere. I was going to stick around and look over my family. I was going to watch my children and watch my wife, and make sure no harm came to them.

"So I stayed in that ghost-like state for five years, watching over them. My wife turned to the church, because she was so grief-stricken and so angry, and she could not forgive these people for having done what they did to me. But eventually she met another man, and when she met that man and they married and the family was taken care of, I then left."

A lifetime of religious and spiritual exploration has led Sims to such things as New Thought beliefs, Religious Science, and the Unity Church, which she now attends regularly. Although she was raised with the traditional ideas of God the father, heaven and hell, sin and salvation, she no longer ascribes to those somewhat limited concepts.

"When I think about God, what I think of is loving presence. I think of beauty.

"I don't think we can fathom the totality of God's creation. I think a lot of people have to create a human figure so we can have some comprehension of an image of him. It's so mind-blowing; it's so unbelievable and hard for us to comprehend. I remember when (Apple founder) Steve Jobs was dying, and the last words he [reportedly] uttered were, 'Wow, wow, wow.' A man like Steve Jobs, who had this incredible brilliant mind and exquisite gift, was blown away by it. So, I think that is what is so exciting, is that we are all going to experience some sort of epiphany when we recognize what type of intelligence we've been created by.

"I do believe there is something there. It's just too much of a miracle for me not to believe in something. It's an idea that is so huge that we can't comprehend it, and I think it's kind of fun that we get to live in this mystery.

"One of my favorite lines from the Bible is, 'It is done unto you as you believe.' What that says is, it gives us the power of choice to create our own belief systems.

"There's another saying—I don't know who came up with it—that says, 'Brainwash yourself first, before somebody nasty beats you to it.' Unfortunately, a lot of brainwashing and nastiness has gone on in which the fire and brimstone, the hell and the sinner, and all of that, has happened. And it has been detrimental, I think, to a lot of people in finding their way back to a place of unconditional love.

"I had to do a lot of reprogramming, and that's why I am grateful to Religious Science and Unity Church, because it helped me reprogram and realize that I'd like to have some beneficial beliefs and see how those work in my life—and they work just fine, thank you."

As for her own death, Sims says she thinks about it, but not in a fearful way. Her sister's untimely death showed her that life is precious, and she tries to make the most of each day as it comes.

"I'm not afraid to die. But like most people, I don't really relish the idea of suffering. There are these advocacy groups working here in Hawaii to try to change the laws to allow for compassionate death, and I watched this beautiful film recently called *How to Die in Oregon*. It was about a woman who suffered with liver cancer, and she went through all the conventional treatments, and it just became a very painful ordeal with no other choices left, and she decided to take Secanol, I believe is the name of the drug.

"You have to be able to administer this to yourself, but you're given a choice. You go through classes, schooling, making sure that you understand that you are choosing to do this. She said, 'You know, I grew up on a farm, and we always put the animals down when they were suffering. Why we won't do that for ourselves is beyond me.'

"Obviously, I would love to go to bed one night and die in my sleep. That would be the ultimate. Or to sit down in a chair at the end of the day and leave my body. But, in cases where that's not possible, I am very interested in advocating for compassionate death, because I think the idea of prolonged suffering is inhumane.

"As far as my death, I think every day is another gift, another day that I've been allowed to live on this planet. So I always think about the fact that any of us could die at any moment. Probably because my sister died so suddenly, I just always feel like every day is another chance to be alive, and I don't know how long . . .

"I guess I'm ready to die. I hope I have more time—there are lots of things I still want to do and accomplish—but I'm willing to surrender to the destiny of whatever my life's plan is."

Chapter 36:

Bruce Welch

> *"I think we either go to heaven or hell, one or the other, because I've read it in the Bible—that Christ is coming back for us and we'll rise and we'll be heading to the heavens with him, man."*

His father's cruel and untimely death not long after he retired from a lifetime of factory work changed the way Georgia resident Bruce Welch looked at the world, and sent him dangerously close to self-destruction.

"Actually, I think I went a little crazy," Welch, a fifty-four-year-old father of three, grandfather of two, and computer tech support specialist, says. "His death (from Lou Gehrig's disease in 2001) had a profound effect on me. For one thing, I guess I figured out that I really did love him more than I thought I did, because of the way my heart felt after he was gone. We had some rough times over the years, and I found out maybe a little too late that I really did love my dad.

"His death was so unfair. He did all this planning and everything else [for his retirement years], and it just didn't come to fruition for him. So I just figured that I'm going to live one day at a time, and do what I need to do to be happy from day to day. I'm not going to plan everything out. I think I'm just going to enjoy life right now and not plan so much for when I retire, you know. Things are just going to be the way they're going to be, and I'm going to enjoy the ride.

"Unfortunately, I went a little bit overboard with it. Just pretty much flirting with disaster."

A lot of that reckless behavior over the next decade or so included alcohol, and it wasn't until his infant grandson was diagnosed with a life-threatening illness that Welch began to take a hard look at what he was doing. He pleaded with God to heal his middle daughter's son in exchange for a promise to straighten out his own life.

"That was really where the alcoholism and God kind of hit face-to-face," said Welch, who was raised as a Catholic, but now considers himself a nondenominational Christian. "I prayed to God and said I would do anything—quit drinking, quit smoking—if he would just heal my grandson. And even when he came out OK, I just kept doing what I was doing. I didn't keep my end of the bargain.

"That eventually hit me straight in the face. I kept thinking about that, and I thought, 'You know, you're pretty shitty not keeping your end of the bargain. I think you need to make some changes.'

"And believe it or not, God worked with me through all that, because he's the one who put the idea in my heart and my mind that I needed to go somewhere like AA or whatever. That I needed help, and that I couldn't do it on my own. So that was intuitively put in my head. I intuitively knew what to do because God told me that I had to go somewhere, and that's the first thing that came to mind. I really believe it was God telling me that."

That was in April 2013, and Welch has been sober ever since. He also has adopted a renewed sense of spirituality and purpose that has improved nearly every aspect of his life. He starts and ends his day now with prayer and tries to center his life around the Bible, which he believes is the word of God.

He believes there is life after death, and that when people die, they go to one of two places: heaven or hell. No question about it.

"Really, my beliefs on that have never faltered. I think we either go to heaven or hell, one or the other, because I've read it in the Bible—that Christ is coming back for us and we'll rise and we'll be heading to the heavens with him, man.

"In the Catholic church, getting there was a little harder than what it actually is, but I believe what the Bible says, and that's pretty much it.

"You know, I have these conversations a lot with people who believe that the Bible is just stories made up, and it's amazing to me that people think that, and then they see God working in their lives.

"For me, absolutely the number one way I've seen God work is Rita and I being together. I think that's a gift from God. I don't think there's another woman in this world who would put up with my shit as much as she has. That, and my struggles with alcohol. God has taken that away from me, basically. The need, the want, the cravings, and all that. And as I go through and start learning more and become more in touch with God, I'm seeing improvements in my life. There's better relationships with other people; I'm-getting-out-of-myself kind of thing. And when I do that, I see changes in other people. So that's how God works, for me."

Although he believes that belief in Jesus and following biblical principles is his ticket to heaven, Welch concedes that is the answer he has found for himself. For someone else, the answer might be different.

"People are different, and I really and truly believe that God is merciful and he really looks at a person's heart. People don't necessarily have to say specific things or do specific things. I think if a person is good in their heart, they're going to get to heaven.

"For me, I believe what the Bible says. And that's why I go that way. I believe it's just a matter of a personal relationship with God. And doing what's right, you know, what God expects of you. I don't think it's hard. I believe that you confess with your mouth that Jesus Christ is Lord, and you live your life according to that, and you pretty much go to heaven. You renounce it, and you're going to hell.

"I pray every day. I pray on my knees in the morning, and I pray on my knees at night. I pray that I can be useful to God in any way that I possibly can.

"I would say I'm more spiritual than religious. I don't believe in the religiosity of things—where you have to repeat things over and over and over again, and that you have to believe a specific way. It's about being good with God, you know what I mean? I think there are all different types of people, and there's all different kinds of things in this world that I can listen to and still hear God's voice. I don't have to go to church to hear that.

"Now, as far as life after death, I absolutely believe in life after death. So, no, I don't have much fear about dying. I don't think about it a whole lot. I guess my time will be up when my time is up. I'll go when I go. I just live my life."

Chapter 37:

Lucía Miguel Bores

> *"I believe human beings have a soul that does not die, but goes on."*

When she arrived at the hospital to see her dying mother one last time, it was too late. But Lucía Miguel Bores says her mother's spirit was still there waiting.

"She died at age seventy-three after a heart operation," Bores recalls. "She was in a coma for one day, and then there was that phone call in the middle of the night, rushing to the hospital . . ."

It was supposed to be a relatively simple heart valve replacement surgery, and everything apparently went well, Bores explained. One day later, things unexpectedly took a turn for the worse.

"My mum was operated [on] on the fifth of January. According to the doctor, everything was OK. She would be sedated for some time, so we could only see her for some minutes in the intensive care unit. The following day (the 'Three Wise Men Day') when we got to the hospital, another doctor told us my mum's condition had gone very serious because of unexpected problems.

"She was in a coma, and we spent the day praying for her to come back; it was the only possible thing to do. As you must know, the visits at the IC unit are very short. I tried to forget about all the tubes and machines connected to my mum, and I talked to her as if she could hear me. I told her that we still had a lot of things to do together. At that time, we had just moved to our house and she hadn't still seen it finished (my parents lived in a town three hundred kilometers away from the village where I live), because she hadn't been feeling well since September. I told her how nice it would be to spend time outside in the garden (we had always lived in flats). In a way, I tried to convince her to fight for her life. But she didn't or she couldn't.

"Then we had to go home for the night, and at around 6 a.m., my phone rang and I drove my brother to hospital. My father (aged seventy-five then) was in bed. We told him we were going to hospital and he wept, 'Has she died?' I remember thinking my dad had become a 'good-for-nothing.' I remember thinking my mum had gone to a better life, to find some peace, and when I saw her without all the tubes and machines, I recognized her. She was calm and beautiful; she was warm when my brother and I kissed her goodbye. I'm sure she was waiting for us. She had told me several times that we—her children—had been the most beautiful part of her life, so there she was once again, for the last time. She was there, still her . . . dead, but she was still my mother, waiting for my brother and me, the last goodbye.

"Two hours later, when I drove my dad to see her, she was very different. She was not her anymore. There was a body, but I could feel her soul had left. Something very difficult to explain, but so real, though. My dad said, 'How beautiful she is,' and, 'She looks as if she's sleeping,' and I remember thinking, 'She's gone; she's not on this world anymore.'

"At that moment, I felt that I changed my 'life category.' I didn't have a mother anymore, but I was—I am—a mother, and I had new responsibilities.

"As I have said, my dad was a very weak person. He lived another five years and died aged eighty-one. Those five years were very hard because my mum was the soul of the family. She was the one who kept us together, so her death was a big loss. But to a certain extent, I do believe she goes on living in me."

Bores, a fifty-one-year-old married mother of two, was born in Irún, Guipúzcoa, Spain. She has a degree in French philology and has been a teacher for twenty-five years.

Her parents were "not very religious," so the family—she, her older brother, and her parents—did not go to church together, but Bores studied Catholicism at school, went to weekly catechism, and attended church with friends on Sunday mornings.

"Spain used to be very Catholic until two decades ago, and that meant religion as a subject at school," she recalls. "I attended a special Mass for children, and the priest was really good at making it interesting and rewarding for us. That period was essential for my future views, although I started to be quite critical about certain official church matters as a teenager.

"Sometimes I went to church and sometimes I did not. It depended on the priest. Now, I go regularly because I love the two priests we have in the village where I live. I am a Catholic, and this is the only church around. I live in a small village of twenty-three hundred people, but we have here two big churches, and we can go to Mass every day if we want to. I only go on Sunday."

She absolutely believes in God and life after death, but Bores says she is not so sure about the reality of a place called heaven and a place called hell. She considers herself more spiritual than religious.

"I believe in God—I would not understand life itself without God's intervention. I am a spiritual person, not religious in the traditional Spanish way, at least not in the traditional way of the region I live, where religious practice is quite superficial, in my opinion. When I think of God, I think of the idea of a loving being a bit like a father/mother, always there even when you can't see them, protecting you, caring for you, telling you off sometimes.

"I am not sure about heaven and hell. I think heaven and hell are already on earth. Life itself is heaven and hell. I reckon these concepts were created to convince people to be good. It is also a way to relieve people when they suffer, making them think they will be made up for all their misery later in heaven.

"In general, when I think about my loved ones who passed away and I want to 'talk' to them, I look up to the sky. I suppose this is because we tend to think that our invisible soul is somehow made of 'air,' floating here and there. But, as I said before, I believe more in a different state than in a place. Heaven is feeling peace inside; hell is eternal dissatisfaction, the inability to be happy.

"For me, it means I must live my life without hurting anyone and, of course, it means I have a soul that makes me different from animals, which also implies big responsibilities. Having said that, I must add that some of my best friends are atheists and behave in the same way as I do.

"I believe human beings have a soul that does not die, but goes on. I think our soul leaves our dead body and lives in a different dimension.

"I did not choose to be born, but I was, in a particular family, in a particular time and place, which, for me, is a sort of miracle. Once I am here, I feel the meaning of my life is to make the best of it . . . we live to learn, to help the people around me to be happy, accomplished, and to make my little world a better place for my children and all the people who will go on living after me."

Bores says she has a good life, and thinks sometimes about death, but does not dwell on it or live in fear of dying.

"It is not a pleasant thought, but the awareness that my time is limited helps me to try to do my best while I'm alive," she says. "I'm more afraid of the physical and psychological suffering that usually goes with it than of dying.

"Obviously when someone close to me dies I think about it, especially if it is a young person. That is more difficult to admit, but again, I imagine we are given a limited time to live—it is a good idea not to tell us how much—and we are free to decide how to spend it, given our personal circumstances and environment.

"From my personal experience you are much happier when you give, when you love, when you help, when you forget a bit about yourself. I often pray to say thank you to God because I consider I have a good life, family, and friends. Sometimes I pray for some special needs, mine or the others. It is quite simple for me. I'm not an expert in theology, but I'm fifty-one now, and I've learnt quite a lot about life. In fact, I'm still learning."

Chapter 38:

Linda Altum

> *"Do I believe in life after death? Yes and no. I'm not sure about the burning in hell part, even though the thought of it is good when you say you want someone to burn in hell!"*

Linda Altum grew up going to church with her mother in Carthage, Missouri. Not only was it a less than pleasant experience, but those weekly services also left her thinking she was doomed for someplace other than singing with angels for all time and eternity.

"We went to Baptist church every Sunday, and it was scary," Altum explains. "The preacher preached hell and damnation, and I just knew I would be bound for hell. I never walked down the aisle and committed because of all the crying, and also because I didn't want to be dunked (baptized) in front of everybody.

"I did not like my Sunday school teacher, either, so when I got older and didn't have to go anymore, I didn't."

Now sixty years old and retired from the public education system, where she spent thirty-three years as a teacher and coach, Altum grew up in Missouri with a twin sister and an older brother. She graduated from Sarcoxie High School and played volleyball at Missouri Southern State University. She is divorced and recently remarried but never had children.

"Just didn't happen," she says of motherhood. "And I'm OK with that. People ask me about it, and I guess I just never had that maternal whatever to miss it.

"I was a stepmother when I was with my husband that had two kids. A damn good one, too. We were married twelve years, so I was in their life for a long time."

Altum says she believes in God, or some sort of "higher power." She has gone to various churches over the years, and around 1990 officially joined a Church of Christ but found the politics at church too much to stomach. So now she is not a regular churchgoer, but she does pray sometimes.

"I talk to God. I look for guidance and help," she says. "It makes me think about things—situations—a little better. I sure could have used this when I was younger—I knew it all back then.

"I don't think it's really necessary to go to church, but then I do think it might keep a person in better touch with God, and I might be more spiritual if I did go regularly."

As for life after death, heaven and hell, all the big questions of life, Altum says yes, no, maybe.

"It's a good question. I want to believe in life after death, but I'm not seeing or feeling it. My first thought is . . . nothing. Everything stops. You don't know it because you're dead! Then let's think about the hereafter—pleasant feelings, tranquility, etc.

"Maybe if there is a hereafter, it is a more pleasant place than this," she says. "If there is some place called heaven, I don't believe we get there as humans, but only our spirit. Again, either in a pleasant place or not so pleasant—but I'm not sure about the burning in hell part, even though the thought is good when you say you want someone to burn in hell!

"I want to believe there is a higher power, some sort of being, God. I do think about it, and I think sometimes about dying. It makes me afraid, so I usually make myself stop thinking about it. I don't want to leave where I am right now.

One of the more traumatic experiences she has had with death and dying was a car crash that killed a sixteen-year-old female cousin.

"I was younger than her, and it was such a shock to have someone so close to you gone forever. Death and bad things were never discussed in our house growing up. We kids did not go to the funeral. I don't know if that would have changed my thoughts and feelings about death or devastated me."

Another influence on her life and her spiritual outlook is a friendship she formed while coaching sports, Altum explained. Even now, she thinks about the example of being a faithful Christian she saw watching her colleague and her husband.

"Sharon McCollister—I coached with her for ten years. She and her husband were in their mid to late thirties when they met and married. They both were virgins, which still just freaking amazes me to this day.

"She grew up Church of Christ, and Jerrod, her husband, grew up Baptist. Just watching them, listening . . . still touches me and makes me think. I am so impressed and proud of them. I truly think she was put in my life for a reason. To open my eyes or to remind me?

"I think we are all put here for a reason. What mark did you make? Will you be remembered? Good, bad, and ugly. And that doesn't mean becoming rich and famous. I think I was meant to be where I am, and I was meant to do what I did and what I am still doing."

Chapter 39:

Stefan Emunds

> *"I'm curious what's on the other side and whether I can level up my spiritual career over there. I'm also curious about who I will meet."*

He used to consider himself an atheist, but fifty-year-old Germany native Stefan Emunds says he banks on God's existence, and not only that, he looks forward to the afterlife.

"I don't *believe* in God; *I know* he exists," says Emunds, a father of four and author of inspirational books, like *God Child*. "I realized that life, planet Earth, and the universe are just too intelligent to be the result of a series of fortunate chemical events. Materialism doesn't make any sense to me. I also sense my eternal existence, which I suppose to be divine.

"I believe that when we die, we withdraw to our mental body, which bears our mind—meaning we carry all our thoughts, feelings, and memories with us. We withdraw to higher planes of existence. Shortly after death, we recap our life experiences (the famous extensive memory picture) and extract the wisdom inherent in it. This could be compared to a long psychoanalytical session, during which we separate our emotions from our experiences and memories.

"It could also be called purgatory, but it's not a punishment, rather an uncomfortable and sometimes painful phase of purification. After the purgatory, we migrate to a place in the afterworld (not the physical universe), where we live until our mental body has withered away, too, which can take centuries. When we drop our mental body, our awareness withdraws to our soul that resides in an even higher realm that is commonly known as *heaven*.

"Hell is a subrealm of the afterworld. Heaven is a complete realm or universe on its own, where we live as souls waiting for the next incarnation. How do we get there? Automatically and with helpers or guides. And here is an important side note: the less people make efforts during planetary life to produce spiritual awareness and consciousness, the less conscious they are in between incarnations. Most people turn 'unconscious' at latest when they drop their mental body and ascend to heaven.

"I'm not afraid of dying at all, because I won't (really) die. I'm a bit worried about my children, though. That would be my only wish: that they will be safe."

Emunds grew up with a Catholic mother and a mostly nonreligious father. He attended a Catholic church, but religion and spirituality was not emphasized at home. He does not have much use for the Catholic Church or any organized religion these days, but he believes in the power of prayer as a way of communicating with God.

"I don't pray in the common sense of the word. I think the common way of 'praying' is uneffective. When people pray, they usually talk about themselves and ask God for this and that. God knows all about them already, so they bore him with repetition. Also, we shouldn't tell God what we want, we should listen instead what he wants for us. He knows what's best for us, and he answers even before we ask. In my book, listening is the proper way of praying, but then it's not called praying anymore.

"My parents never taught me religion, nor philosophy, not to talk about spirituality. It had a good side though: I grew up without anyone telling me what to think and what not, in respect to religion and philosophy, I mean.

"When I was sixteen, I joined a philosophy class at school. That opened my eyes, and I became an atheist. When I was twenty-one, I joined a spiritual organization, and that opened my eyes a second time, and I became a spiritual person. I need to add that these two events didn't change me; the change occurred gradually over time as a result of study and research.

"I studied so much about religion and spirituality . . . and now, Catholic dogmas appear at best crude and at worst simply wrong. I cannot relate anymore—in particular, their notion of people living just one time on this particular planet and then going for the rest of the universe's existence (googolplexes of years) to a heaven or hell is simply nonsense. We're not just drops of water falling on a hot stone and, *zssht*, we're gone again.

"I think the purpose of life is to experience joy, adventures, and learning how to have a better life, meaning how to have more joy, more intensive experiences, and greater adventures. God created the world, and we experience it for him, something he could never do. There's glory in our adventures and, in this respect, we are of incredible value to God.

"Having said that, I feel death is going to be a relief, a well-deserved break. I want to be fully awake when it happens. I feel like doing one more great thing before I pass away. I'm curious what's on the other side, and whether I can level up my spiritual career over there. I'm also curious about who I will meet."

Chapter 40:

Dr. Heather Rivera

> *"I am not afraid. I already experienced my past-life deaths and realized that I don't really die. I am only an awareness in a Heather suit, and next time, I may be in a Henry suit."*

Dying and whatever happens after that does not concern California native Heather Friedman Rivera in the least.

Why? Because she has died many times before and she knows exactly what comes next.

"I believe we meet with soul groups, look over our life, decide what lessons we learned and what we still need to learn, and choose our next incarnation," Dr. Rivera says.

In other words, when we die, we soon come back to life in another form, another body. A different person. Another life, another chance.

Reincarnation.

It was during an impromptu visit to a hypnotherapist in 2008 that Dr. Rivera got an up close and personal look at reincarnation. She decided that day, for whatever reason, to try hypnosis on a whim, very skeptical but also curious. When she left the therapist's office a short time later, her life was forever changed.

"You know how you're going down a boardwalk or something and there's a palm reader, and you think, 'Oh, that'd be fun.' That's the same idea I had to see this therapist," the fifty-one-year-old registered nurse and mother of three from Santa Monica explained. "I just wanted some entertainment and to laugh about it later. I didn't even think I could be hypnotized.

"During the session, I found myself in a knight's body. I was wearing armor, and I felt hungry and cold from the damp air . . . I could think all his thoughts, and yet I could also think Heather's thoughts at the same time. We progressed into the next significant event in that lifetime, and I was in battle, and I was stabbed in the throat. I was coughing and choking on blood, and I was also coughing and choking in the chair in the therapist's office.

"I remember I was holding on to my shield or my sword. My hands were tightly clenched, and then I finally took my last breath as a knight, and I felt myself rise out of that body. My hands relaxed and then I became very expansive and really huge and felt this connection with everybody and everything. I had this incredible sense of love and peace and just . . . awareness that our bodies are not who we really are. We're just having incarnations multiple times.

"Then she (the therapist) called me back, and I went back into Heather's body, and I had this ongoing physical healing that has been continuous and hasn't gone away. I actually had to take some time off from work to process everything I now thought about life and death, God, purpose.

"That was the first spiritual experience of my life, and I had no idea that everything would change after that. I just got obsessed with past life after that day."

Her experience was so profound, in fact, that Dr. Rivera soon pursued and completed a doctoral dissertation on past-life experiences, earned a PhD in parapsychic science from the American Institute of Holistic Theology, and now is a highly regarded past-life researcher, speaker, and writer, in addition to her nursing duties. She also holds a degree in law.

As a child, she was raised in the Jewish faith and attended synagogue, but never really connected with the religion of her parents.

"I liked the food and music, but the religion part didn't really resonate with me," she says. "I just didn't feel like I belonged."

As time went on, Dr. Rivera became "pretty much an atheist" before discovering Buddhism in 1997. She felt comfortable with those teachings, and then there was that amazing day in the hypnotist's chair. And after that, she went on to experience what is referred to as "life between lives regression," described as a healing journey back in time. Using hypnosis, it takes one back through pleasant childhood experiences, into the womb all the way back into a past life or lives to explore significant and meaningful events. Life purpose and other profound questions are examined through meetings with loved ones, soul guides, and others.

"You skip the past life part, and you go to your life when you're in the spirit world," Dr. Rivera explains. "You learn what your purpose is, lessons you learned in your past life, and you prepare for your new life, including which body you're going to pick.

"They took me to, like, a boardroom, and I asked questions. I saw the image of a cross, which really was kind of disturbing to me at that point, because it wasn't what I was raised with. So I said, 'What am I supposed to do?' or something like that. And my guide said, 'Buddha's love, Jesus's love, and your love is all the same love.' He was acknowledging Buddha and Jesus, but also me as being part of that. And he said, 'Whatever you do with love and intention, that is your purpose.'"

Today, Dr. Rivera feels most closely aligned with the principles of Buddhism, although she also believes in God, due to her experience in the life between lives regression. Not the more traditional view of God, perhaps, like the one found in the Christian Bible, but some sort of supreme being, nonetheless. And in no way does she criticize others for their own beliefs.

"I think that's fine for them. One thing that I've learned is that I'm not Heather, and I'm not the knight, and I'm not that servant girl, and I'm not that monk. I've been many things, so it's easy for me to appreciate all other cultures and religions, because I've been all of them. I don't feel like I can pigeonhole myself into any one thing anymore.

"I'm not sure I believed in God as a child, but as an adult, I've had experiences in meditation and hypnosis that led me to believe there is a God. Or to be more accurate, we are all one in God. When I think of God, I think of one force of love that we are all a part of, and maybe part of us never left. Only a piece of us is having this earthly experience.

"I don't go to a church or synagogue today, and I rarely visit a Buddhist temple. I'm not religious, but I am spiritual. I find that nature is the closest to God that I can get. And I do believe we create our own heaven and hell by our intention, attitude, and choices."

Needless to say, all of these experiences have removed any fear of death or dying, Mrs. Rivera says. After this life, she will simply move on to the next.

"I am not afraid. I already experienced my past life deaths and realized that I don't really die. After the knight experience, I feel like I'm immortal. I am only an awareness in a Heather suit and next time I may be in a Henry suit.

"I speak all over the place, and I have books published on this subject. I've been on syndicated radio all over the country, and I hear people say, like the radio announcer, he's like, 'Aw, c'mon, Doc, do you really believe in past lives?' I hear that all the time, and that's OK. I'm from California, after all," she says, laughing. "So it's OK."

Chapter 41:

Kenya Cluff

> *"I was instantly pulled into heaven. . . . God said, in a loud, discerning voice: 'It's not your time, Kenya.' Cliché, I know, but that's what he said."*

Encounters with spirits were nothing new for Oregonian Kenya Cluff, but during a surgical procedure in 2013, she experienced the most remarkable meeting of her life.

"It was January 14," Cluff says. "I was still in the hospital healing after my first surgery on the seventh, and I started having severe spasms, so they took me back under to find out what was going on.

"I broke my back twice in skydiving and skateboarding accidents, so I had screws and a cage put in my spine. Well, they ended up taking out a screw on the fourteenth. While I was under anesthesia was the next best day of my life. I woke from surgery in the recovery room, pulling out my own breathing tube with a huge smile on my face. I couldn't wait to tell everyone what just happened."

What happened, she says, is that she underwent a near-death experience and actually traveled to a place she believes was heaven.

"It starts like this—in front of me was clouds that went on forever, and to my left was a golden arch and golden fence that clearly I wasn't able to go through yet. I looked to the right and there's a long line of gray people, meaning it was like their souls were there, all in line against a fence. I looked at the arch, where an indescribably bright light was shining, unlike anything I'd seen before.

"It was God, and he said in a loud discerning voice: 'It's not your time, Kenya.' Cliché, I know, but that's what he said.

"I look in front of me, and I'm on a gravel rectangle and can't leave that spot. To my left is my dad in his red shirt and jeans. He said, 'Tell Nancy (my mom) to stop worrying; I'm always with her.' In the middle was an angel named Cassidy, who was my daughter I never got to raise because she died in the womb at five months. She said to tell my other daughter that she can't wait to meet her and soon. Scary, I try not to think about that too much.

"And to my right was my best friend, my dog, who came up and licked my leg. Then, [he went] back to his gravel spot—like a rug—where he obviously couldn't wait to go because he kept looking over there, panting.

"I was then turned around and was gliding through the most amazing garden imaginable, rolling green mossy terrain—not grass—trees everywhere in colors you've never seen before, and a beautiful river that ran through it. I went down a cinder-looking path, with nothing in front of me, and I woke up.

"So, do I believe in life after death? Do I believe in God, and in heaven? Absolutely."

Cluff, a forty-year-old divorced mother of four and grandmother of seven, grew up with a brother and three sisters in a nonreligious family. With "no Godly parenting whatsoever," she did not go to church much as a child and does not attend now, but she has been exposed to several different Christian denominations, including Mormon and Lutheran.

As a young girl, she experienced visits from what she considered evil spirits, and these visits continued into her adult years. She was naturally frightened every time, but also convinced that if there were such a thing as evil—that she was witnessing firsthand—there also must be such a thing as good.

"I just always knew, since I was little—like two to six years old—that if there was bad, there was also good. I had no proof; I just knew there had to be.

"It wasn't until I was six that I told my mother about any of it. I was playing in the garage, which was our play room, and I was sitting with my doll, when a big clothes bin—like a tall wine barrel—knocked over and rolled back and forth from one end of the garage to the other, several times.

"We didn't have animals; there was no draft; no way it was earthly. I was so terrified . . . I ran in and told my mom. She said I was making it up and told me to go play. I had many of these type of experiences before age twenty.

"As an adult, my husband and I were sitting in our kitchen when we were visited by three entities that we played with—asking questions and telling them to change forms, which they did. One night that same year, when I was twenty-two, I woke up lying next to my husband, with a dark, black-cloaked figure, almost like in the Harry Potter movie, lying on top of me, holding me down.

"My husband saw this, so we picked up my daughter and drove to the butte and slept that night in the car. I had bruises the next day on my wrist. We had [people from] the church over the following Sunday to come pray over our home. I told them to go to my closet, where my clothes often flew around by the hangers, and it actually happened as the thirty church members witnessed it. Eventually, we moved from there.

"About two years later, I was driving my car when all the windows fogged up and the gas pedal accelerated. I looked in the rearview mirror and there's several faces imaged in the foggy windows. I prayed as hard as I could and the windows cleared up. I went to church the following Sunday and there was a spiritual healer there, one of those hands-on people who touch you and you fall over flushed with the spirit. I was skeptical but curious, so I went up to the pew and, along with ten others, I was pushed down by a flood of wind. I went back to my seat and was just in awe as I stared out the window and saw my first and only angel—just the brightest, most beautiful winged lady.

"'Finally,' I thought, 'the proof.' Physical proof. I always knew there was a God. That's when all the dark spirits harassing me stopped."

All those experiences combined have led Cluff to a place where she is not afraid of death, because she "know[s] where [she's] going." She prays regularly and believes that her prayers are answered.

"I prayed and prayed about why I didn't die that day in the hospital, and I decided after that, my real purpose is simply this: to learn, to love, to have faith, to trust in God and his power to get us through any obstacle.

"Nothing happens for no reason. We are where we are supposed to be for reasons we don't need to understand. Life will offer good and bad options, and it's up to us to learn why—to choose to be good or strive to be good.

"No one is perfect. I'm absolutely not angry, not on drugs, not depressed; for I accept this position in life right now to be for reasons I may not understand.

"I pray religiously. All day long, little prayers. When I'm going through hard times, I ask for specific guidance and, amazingly, it's quickly answered."

Conclusion

What an amazing experience.

Heartfelt thanks go out once again to everyone who participated in this effort, allowing me to interview them and sharing their highly personal thoughts and fascinating beliefs about one of life's biggest mysteries—what happens next?

As was the case in my first book about religious and spiritual issues, I was truly humbled by the openness and honesty in all these conversations, proving to me once again that despite differences in such things as background, culture, religion, age, education, and socioeconomic status, people across not only the United States, but around the world, are basically all the same inside. Everyone wants pretty much the same things out of life, I think: love, security, happiness.

I daresay that if "the folks" had their way, peace would break out all over the planet tomorrow.

I consider myself a seeker, looking for answers, but not yet deciding in my hearts of hearts what I truly believe about things like God and life after death. After six or seven years of what I will call "indoctrination" as a kid, attending a Christian church and going to Sunday school meetings, youth group on Wednesday nights, all that, I think I believe that life probably does go on somehow after we die.

Growing up, I was taught that there is God, his son, Jesus, and something called the Holy Ghost. I'm not too sure what the Holy Ghost does, but I think he or she is some sort of messenger.

There is a wonderful place called heaven where they all live, and a horrible place called hell, where Satan lives. When you die, you stand before God as he reviews the events of your life, both good and bad, and counts up the strikes against you that have been recorded through the years in some type of book of life. I remember someone teaching that reviewing your life would be just like a movie, with everyone watching, presumably on a very big screen.

How embarrassing and shameful.

In the end, if you racked up enough sins during your lifetime, you are sent to hell. If not, you get to live in heaven.

I was scared to death of God.

At about age fifteen, I told my dad one Sunday morning that I was not going to church. We argued about it, but he gave up and let me stay home. I never went again.

Over the next twenty years or so, I committed enough sins to fill at least a good-size chapter of that Book of Life. I tried going to church a few times in my early thirties, and then again in my late forties. I even got baptized in a lake and served as a church trustee during a three-year stint in which I also played guitar in the praise and worship band. I gave it my best shot, but just could never really buy into it all.

For one thing, I have a big problem with the whole Bible story. Here is my view on that in a nutshell: if God—who is really Jesus, and vice versa—is all knowing and all loving, the epitome and essence of pure love, how could he possibly send any of his children to burn in hell for eternity? Who would do such a thing? Not only that, if he is all knowing, all seeing, he knows before our lives even begin how things are going to turn out. So he knows before we are even born whether we are going to screw it all up and go to hell when we die.

What kind of setup is that?

If the Bible is true, then hell must be a really big place, because according to common interpretation of the scriptures, anyone who does not believe and profess that God's son, Jesus Christ, died on the cross for the forgiveness of sin and to make it possible to live with God in heaven, is doomed to an eternal sentence in hell.

Lots and lots of people do not ascribe to that belief. Me included.

The end times, when Jesus is supposed to return and rule the Earth for a thousand years or something, has been right around the corner for a long, long time, and I'm just not buying that one, either.

If God is up there, out there, over there, somewhere, watching daily events unfold, why in the world would he let so much incredible pain and suffering go on? Why allow horrible things to happen to wonderful people? Innocent people? Kids? Babies?

It's all part of God's plan, "they" say. Really? Well, that's a pretty rotten plan, if you ask me.

I thought Brett Sailors's description of God as "an all-powerful being apparently responsible for the favorable outcome of many major sporting events" was pretty hilarious. Irreverent, sure, but funny. I liked Vanessa Rivera's unique image of life after death as a never-ending sleep with dreams so pleasant that we never want to wake up. Koi Hatchootucknee says he routinely communicates with spirits from the other side, wherever that is, and I have no reason to not believe him. Dr. Heather Rivera (no relation to Vanessa) and Susanne Sims have vivid recollections of past lives and deaths. Brooke Lewis has seen ghosts or spirits up close and personal, as have members of her family.

I have read that a measurable amount of weight and energy leaves the body at the time of death, and science says that energy does not disappear. Some say that energy at the time of death is the soul leaving the body. Could be, I suppose. Kind of makes sense. If so, where does it go?

I would like to think that there is some place where supreme joy abounds for all time—no problems, no pain, no worries—and we are reunited with our loved ones, basking in God's love and light. How wonderful it would be to see my mother again, my grandmothers and grandfathers, old friends. Sounds pretty far-fetched, though, honestly. And I definitely don't believe in hell. Heaven? Maybe. Hell? No way.

But that is only one view of life after death. There are so many others, as we've seen in this book.

Reincarnation sounds a little far-fetched to me, too, but who's to say it does not happen? That could explain a lot of things, if you think about it.

As far as my own death, I used to think about that a lot, and the idea was always tremendously sad and depressing. I used to think—and still do, in a way—that life is mostly a sad journey, with no happy ending. Let's face it: dying is not a happy ending to the story, and that's the way it always turns out. I hate movies in which the main character, or one of the main characters, dies at the end. I always think, why couldn't they have written the ending a different way?

There was one exception to this, when I saw the movie, *Million Dollar Baby*, starring Hillary Swank and Clint Eastwood. Swank was a female boxer managed by Eastwood, and after coming from a horrible background and upbringing to earn a chance to fight for a world championship, she tragically suffered a broken neck and permanent, total paralysis. In the end, she died, but this time, I wasn't saddened by it as much. For some reason, her death seemed heroic, in a way. I told someone that I thought it was because she made it to the top; she reached her dream.

My thoughts about my own death have changed somewhat in the past year or so, as well. Like a lot of people have said, I ain't ready to go just yet, but when the time comes, I think it will be OK. I've had a pretty darned good life—certainly an interesting one, full of ups and downs, twists and turns, laughter and tears, pain and happiness, joy and sorrow.

I have screwed up a lot of things, but I've also done a lot of things right. And I've achieved some big goals, reached some big dreams, not the least of which is becoming a published author. I never would have imagined it one year ago, but this will likely be my seventh published book, and I think it may be the best one yet. I have traveled overseas—another thing I never imagined doing—and walked one of the world's most famous and historic pilgrimages. I climbed the Pyrenees mountains. My traveling is not nearly as extensive as some folks', but one of my big goals is to spend a year touring the world, just me and a backpack. I fully plan to achieve that goal, too.

I graduated from college, earned a degree, and became a journalist. I interviewed generals, governors, senators, presidents, and covered historic events. After that, I decided to become a school teacher, and I did that.

Although I'm kind of a mess in some ways—moody, insecure, depressive—I love life. Life is beautiful, and, unfortunately, some day it will end.

So, what is going to happen after I die? I really don't know. Like Vanessa, I wonder how many people will miss me. How many will think well of me, and how many will just kind of shrug their shoulders and say, "Oh, that's too bad," or whatever.

I saw another movie where one of the characters was riddled with terminal cancer, and he decided to have his funeral *before* he died. He wanted to hear what people would say about him. I wouldn't mind that. Seeing who shows up and what people have to say.

If it's true that life goes on somehow, maybe I'll be there watching regardless.

Get My Books FREE

Visit my website www.johnclarkbooks.com, and subscribe to my mailing list to get all of my new releases for free. I plan to write many books over the coming years, and I'd love to repay you for taking an interest in my work by allowing you to access all of my future work at no charge. When each new book is released, I'll send you an email with a link to the free book. No strings attached and nothing for sale, ever. Subscribe today at: www.johnclarkbooks.com

A Small Favor to Ask

Thanks for reading this collection; I hope you found these stories meaningful or helpful in some way. If you did, please take just a moment to write a brief review on Amazon of the book. Your reviews mean a great deal to me, and they help others find this book, so that more readers can read these stories and perhaps find some resonance with their own experience, and answers of their own.

About the Author

John Henry Clark III is an award-winning journalist, freelance writer, author, and avid golfer who was born and raised in Texas. He grew up in northwest Houston playing sports at Oaks Dads Club and attending church with his parents, but decided as he got older that things he learned in Sunday school no longer made much sense.

Since then, he has spent a lifetime seeking answers and exploring a variety of beliefs. After a successful career as a newspaper reporter, Clark turned his lifetime love for learning into a new career as a public school teacher, and that gave him time during the summer months to pursue his project to research and write a book describing what people believe about God and why they believe what they believe.

That effort turned into this book, *Finding God*. A tireless seeker, researcher and questioner, John has written a number of other fascinating books dealing with the human experience, from tragedies to triumphs and more, including *Camino: Laughter and Tears along Spain's 500-mile Camino de Santiago*. To read more of John's books, find answers to the meaning of life, and maybe discover something new about yourself, go here: http://amzn.to/1EmgWa7

Printed in Great Britain
by Amazon